Working Together for Local Integration of Migrants and Refugees in Rome

This document, as well as any data and any map included herein, are without prejudice to the status of or sovereignty over any territory, to the delimitation of international frontiers and boundaries and to the name of any territory, city or area.

Please cite this publication as:
OECD (2019), *Working Together for Local Integration of Migrants and Refugees in Rome*, OECD Publishing, Paris.
https://doi.org/10.1787/ca4d491e-en

ISBN 978-92-64-52653-2 (print)
ISBN 978-92-64-92972-2 (pdf)

The statistical data for Israel are supplied by and under the responsibility of the relevant Israeli authorities. The use of such data by the OECD is without prejudice to the status of the Golan Heights, East Jerusalem and Israeli settlements in the West Bank under the terms of international law.

Photo credits: Cover © Marianne Colombani.

Corrigenda to OECD publications may be found on line at: *www.oecd.org/about/publishing/corrigenda.htm*.
© OECD 2019

You can copy, download or print OECD content for your own use, and you can include excerpts from OECD publications, databases and multimedia products in your own documents, presentations, blogs, websites and teaching materials, provided that suitable acknowledgement of OECD as source and copyright owner is given. All requests for public or commercial use and translation rights should be submitted to *rights@oecd.org*. Requests for permission to photocopy portions of this material for public or commercial use shall be addressed directly to the Copyright Clearance Center (CCC) at *info@copyright.com* or the Centre français d'exploitation du droit de copie (CFC) at *contact@cfcopies.com*.

Foreword

When it comes to migrant integration, the local level matters. Where migrants go and how they integrate into their new communities crucially depends on the specific characteristics of cities and regions. Even though migration policies are often under the responsibility of national governments, the concentration of migrants in cities, and particularly in metropolitan areas, has an impact on the local demand for work, housing, goods and services that local authorities have to manage. Local authorities therefore play a vital role in this integration. Cities can learn from each other and help provide local, regional, national and international policy makers and practitioners with better evidence for policy design related to migrant integration.

This case study *Working Together for Local Integration of Migrants and Refugees in Rome* provides insight into the city's migrant integration trends and current situation. It applies the OECD *Checklist for public action to migrant integration at the local level* that is articulated around 4 blocks and 12 objectives. The four blocks cover: 1) institutional and financial settings; 2) time and proximity as keys for migrants and host communities to live together; 3) enabling conditions for policy formulation and implementation; and 4) sectoral policies related to integration: access to the labour market, housing, social welfare and health, and education.

This case study, which is part of a broader OECD-European Union project, entitled "A territorial approach to migrant integration: The role of local authorities", addresses a critical knowledge gap on migration issues by analysing the multi-level governance issues of local integration. The project takes stock of multi-level governance frameworks and policies for migrant and refugee integration at the local level in nine large European cities: Amsterdam, Athens, Barcelona, Berlin, Glasgow, Gothenburg, Paris, Rome and Vienna and, thanks to the support of the German Ministry for Economic Affairs and Energy, a small city in Germany (Altena). It also builds on information from these and 61 other European cities, that were collected through a survey and consolidated into a newly created and publicly available statistical database on migrant integration outcomes at regional level. The project looks at updates to the governance mechanisms that cities adopted in the wake of the influx of asylum seekers and refugees that has concerned EU countries since 2015. Conversely, it also investigates opportunities to extend some of the services recently established for newcomers to long-standing migrant groups.

This and the other nine city case studies, along with the synthesis report *Working Together for Local Integration of Migrants and Refugees,* are outputs of this OECD-European Union initiative contributing to the programme of work of the OECD Regional Development Policy Committee (RDPC), implemented by the Centre for Entrepreneurship, SMEs, Regions and Cities (CFE). They also contribute to the OECD Horizontal Project on "Ensuring the effective integration of vulnerable migrant groups", by focusing on improving the integration capacities of the local governments.

Acknowledgements

This publication *Working Together for Local Integration of Migrants and Refugees in Rome* was produced by the Centre for Entrepreneurship, SMEs, Regions and Cities (CFE) led by Lamia Kamal-Chaoui, Director. It is part of a wider project "A territorial approach to migrant integration: The role of local authorities" and an output of an OECD-European Union (EU) initiative contributing to the programme of work of the OECD's Regional Development Policy Committee (RDPC).

Co-ordination of the wider project and this case study was led by Claire Charbit, Head of the Territorial Dialogue and Migration Unit in the CFE's Regional Development and Tourism Division, managed by Alain Dupeyras. This case study was drafted by Anna Piccinni, Policy Analyst (OECD), based on inputs provided by Carlotta Fioretti (Roma Tre University). It also received substantive additional inputs and contributions from Paola Proietti (OECD). This case study benefitted from the comments of other colleagues across the OECD, including in particular from Jonathan Chaloff from the International Migration Division of the Directorate for Employment, Labor and Social Affairs (ELS).

The case study has been produced thanks to the close collaboration of the Municipality of Rome that provided information and organised the OECD fieldwork (March 2017). While some information regarding legislative changes that took place at national level in late 2018 and early 2019 have been updated, this case study does not reflect how these changes may impact reception and integration activities at the local level. The Secretariat would like to express its gratitude to all the participants to the interviews (see page 73) and in particular to the staff of the municipality: Sabina de Luca, Annalisa Gonizzi and Giancarlo De Fazio, who co-ordinated the interaction with the OECD team, and to the Department of Social Policies, Subsidiarity and Health and the Department of Tourism, training and work who provided substantial information. In addition, the OECD would like to thank the national government representatives – Flavia Terribile, from the Presidency of the Council of Ministers, who made the study possible and the Directorate General of Immigration and Integration Policies of the Ministry of Labour and Social Policies for their comments.

The Secretariat is especially thankful to the EU Directorate General for Regional and Urban Policy (DG Regio) for the financial contribution and the collaboration throughout the implementation of the project of. In particular, the Secretariat would like to thank Andor Urmos for its guidance during this project.

Table of contents

Abbreviations and acronyms 6

Executive summary 7
   Key findings 8

Chapter 1. Key data on migrant presence and integration in Rome 15
   Key Statistics 17
   Migration flows 19
   Migration legal framework (See 0) 21
   Notes 22

Chapter 2. The Checklist for public action to migrant integration at the local level applied to the city of Rome 23
   Block 1: Multi-level governance: Institutional and financial settings 24
   Block 2. Time and space: Keys for migrants and host communities to live together 47
   Block 3. Local capacity for policy formulation and implementation 51
   Block 4: Sectoral Measures 54
   Notes 66
   References 68
   Additional Reading 72
   Annex A: List of participants to the interviews with OECD delegation field visit March 22-24 2017 73
   Annex B National legislative framework for Migration and Asylum 75

Tables

Table 1.1. Foreign residents in the City of Rome (Roma Capitale) 20

Figures

Figure 1.1. Cittá Metropolitana di Roma Capitale (equivalent to the TL3 area) 17
Figure 1.2. Percentage of foreign population over total population per district, 2015 21
Figure 2.1. Institutional Mapping of migrant and refugee integration in Rome 35

Boxes

Box 1.1. Definition of migrant and refugee 16
Box 2.1. A checklist for public action to migrant integration at the local level 24
Box 2.2. Examples of semi-autonomous houses for refugees in Rome 47
Box 2.3. Examples of associations providing support to migrants in Rome 49
Box 2.4. The San Gallicano Hospital and the National Institute for Migrant Health Promotion 61

Abbreviations and acronyms

AMAR	Rome housing mediation agency (Agenzia mediazione abitativa Roma)
AMIF	European Asylum Migration and Integration Fund
ASL	Local Health District (Azienda Sanitaria Locale)
CAAT	Temporary Housing Centres (CAAT, Centri di Assistenza Alloggiativa Temporanea)
CFP	Centre for Vocational Training (Centri di formazione professionale)
CTI	Territorial Council for Immigration (Consigli Territoriali per l'Immigrazione)
CPIA	Adult provincial education centres (Centri provonciali per l'istruzione degli adulti)
CPI	Employment Centre (Centri per l'impiego)
COL	Job orientation centres (Centri orientamento al lavoro)
CSOs	Civil society organisations
DSPSH	Department of Social Policies, Subsidiarity and Health or Social Policy Department of the City of Rome
ERF	European Refugee Fund
EIF	European Integration fund
ENI	"EU citizen not enrolled in the Health system" (Europeo non iscritto,)
INPS	National Welfare institute (Istituto Nazionale della Previdenza Sociale)
PNA	National Asylum Programme (Programma Nazional Asilo)
SSN	National Health System (Sistema Sanitario Nazionale)
STP	Migrants in transit (Stranieri Temporaneamente Presenti)
SPRAR	Protection System for Asylum and Refugee (Sistema di Protezione per Richiedenti Asilo e Rifugiati)

Executive summary

Migrant-related issues have been tackled in Italy and in Rome since the 1990s. The foreign-born population living in Italy has multiplied by fourteen between 1990 and 2015, from above 350 000 in 1991 to about five million in 2015, turning Italy from a country of emigration into a country of immigration. Rome is a migration hub and the biggest city in Italy for number of migrants, with close to 380 000 foreign residents in 2017 coming from 183 different countries (Roma Capitale 2017). Most of the migrants transit in the city, though sometimes it can take years, before continuing their journey, often towards northern European destinations. Although since 1990 an articulated national legislative framework for *migrant* integration has been developed, it still struggles to fully translate into a comprehensive and co-ordinated implementation of integration policies, and the vision for *migrant* inclusion has remained fragmented both at local and national level. Initially focussing primarily on overcoming early obstacles related to reception and registration, the Italian public response increasingly mainstreamed integration-related measures across different policy sectors including health, housing, work, education, participation in social and public life, support to family reunification, etc.

Since the early 2000s, reception and early integration of *asylum seekers and refugees* have been articulated through a co-ordinated and multi-level protection system (the SPRAR). Since 2015, however, Italy has experienced a rapid increase in arrivals: 180 000 new arrivals reached Italian shores in 2016, and in January 2016, 15 000 non-EU newcomers were registered in the Metropolitan City of Rome either as asylum seekers, refugees or subsidiary protection status holders. In order to enlarge the capacity of the SPRAR system, the Italian government established a parallel emergency reception system (CAS) with looser standards in terms of co-ordination with local authorities and early integration measures. In addition, NGOs and faith-based organisations are omnipresent in both areas, reception and long-term integration. Historically, they have generated a myriad of solutions, adapting rapidly to changing local needs. Non-state actors intervene in support of migrants and refugees, either fulfilling their own mandates or implementing services outsourced by the city of Rome.

Lack of cross-levels policy tools and funding to coherently address integration issues has to be understood in the framework of the economic situation of Italian host communities and fiscal constraints. Public resources for social services for all citizens have decreased significantly in recent years. For instance between 2006 and 2016, the National Fund for Social Policy's (FNPS) budget decreased by almost 40% - from EUR 825 million in 2006 to EUR 311 million in 2016. Similarly, in Rome funding for social services decreased by 6.1% - from EUR 366 million in 2012 to EUR 344 million in 2014. At the same time, the demand for social services by poor and homeless national groups increased by 5% between 2012 and 2013.

Following the principle of universal access to public services, most of the actions developed by the sub-national administration - and described in this report - are not migrant-specific, but apply to all residents based on their level of vulnerability.

Regional and local authorities are in charge of the implementation of critical integration-related measures, including services for accessing the labour market, health and adult education. Their action is framed by the availability of resources: allocated either by the national government, collected locally, received from foundations and charities, or from EU funding.

In the absence of a city-wide strategy for migrant integration, measures are often emergency-driven. The increase of arrivals in 2015 contributed to 'revealing' the city's long-standing housing and social exclusion challenges regardless of the specific recipient categories in Rome's population.

Key findings

Some of the remaining challenges

- In Rome, as is the case in most of the European cities studied, **the passage from the reception system** (SPRAR or CAS), where newcomers are initially hosted, to universal services and public administration procedures **can be very problematic**. Among other reasons (i.e. insufficient social housing availability, low local staff capacity, etc), this might also be due to weak multi-level co-ordination: the different reception and integration policies typically follow separate funding and management lines. These circumstances lead migrants, including recognised refugees, to turn increasingly to associations, informal networks and sometimes to live in informal settlements in the city. *Improve the links between targeted and universal services could be beneficial. Rome could consider practices adopted in other EU cities for strengthening recognised refugees' effective passage towards accessing universal services, such as the programme implemented by the city of Amsterdam, which pairs one municipal case worker for every 30 refugees during the first three years since recognition.*

- Although all foreigners, including asylum seekers, have the right to access health and social services in the municipality, where they register as residents, there might be discontinuities in effectively accessing this right. The evidence collected from this case study points to **a possible lack of accompanying mechanisms during the process of enrolling in the municipal residence registry**, with implications for finding housing and a job. Innovative solutions such as the 'Residenze Fittizie' practice have been proposed as an example to other cities, however, their accessibility and sustainability should be monitored. *Better availability of information and adapted mechanisms should be in place to guide migrants during the process of enrolling in the municipal registry.*

- **Provision of Italian language classes for adults in Rome just covers the need of 60-70% of the foreign resident population**. At the same time, individuals must learn Italian in order to obtain their residence permit (Integration Agreement). In addition, the existing offer in Rome relies mainly on actions carried out by Italian NGOs that have organised themselves in the network *'Scuolemigranti'*. A more performant public language teaching system would enable migrants to fulfil more easily their obligation to learn Italian set by law, and is therefore crucial to integrate in the local society. *A well-developed local mechanism for language training is the one implemented by the city of Stockholm that offers 11 language course geared to the future sector of employment of the newcomers. To respond to growing educational needs, public services could also strengthen co-ordination across* *levels of government (Ministry of Education, the Region and the Municipality), in particular for identifying available resources (EU, national and municipal funding) for teaching and formulating a shared programming cycle and indicators.*

- **The city of Rome still needs to develop a clear vision and related communication strategy** with regard to integration actions and the contribution that migrants bring to local development. In a context, where the public discourse on migration has been focused primarily on security, *the municipality could ease tensions by communicating, in a sensitive way, on actions that have been taken to improve reception and integration, and developing narratives on the positive contributions that migrants make to the city. In this sense, the examples of the communication strategies adopted in Berlin, Paris and Barcelona could be helpful.*

- **Housing, and in particular social housing, is highly problematic in Rome** for the entire city population, i.e. foreigners and Italians. Beneficiaries of international protection, as well as other migrants, often find it hard to access decent living conditions. The 2015 peak in arrivals led to an increased number of migrants living in squats and spontaneous settlements; around 3 000 asylum seekers and refugees were estimated to be in this situation in 2016. This emergency revealed structural shortages in public housing that have not been addressed through a local policy since the 1980s. *Beyond emergency measures, the city should invest in long-term public housing, which is one of its competences, and develop projects aiming at the well-being of all inhabitants and vulnerable households in particular. The city of Gothenburg offers interesting examples in terms of long-term housing plans that aim at increasing the social mix and include migrant groups in their reflection to avoid further segregation.*

What is already being done and what could be improved

- **Policy coherence at local level**: Since 1993, Rome's City Council ensures access for migrants to universal welfare and health services (see page 59) as a result of the application of national and regional laws, as well as through specific municipal integration projects. Most services are formally accessible for resident foreigners in areas such as reception, education, vocational orientation, culture, etc. However, the city's overall approach to integration remains rather fragmented and heterogeneous. *In this regard, a 'road-map' approach to mainstream integration standards that ensure access for migrants and refugees across all sectors could be helpful. Some cities analysed through this study have developed more systematic strategies (such as Vienna, Barcelona, Amsterdam, etc), by designing bridges among service providers to ensure migrants' access to various universal services in a consistent way.*

- **Political oversight of the city's approach to integration**. In particular since 2015, most of the cities analysed in this study, have scaled up or established municipal department/ entity with clear competences and resources for migrant and refugee integration (Vienna, Amsterdam, Barcelona, etc). Other municipalities appointed a vice-mayor (Athens), a Commissioner (Berlin), or an advisor (Gothenburg) for migration and refugees at the highest executive level. In Rome, the Social Policies Department has established several 'technical co-ordination offices' for integration-related topics (i.e. technical office for reception, labour, etc.) or specific groups (i.e. unaccompanied minors, Roma, etc.) as described on page 36. This is a quite unique practice for sharing information and seeking coherence across departments; however, its efficiency needs to be tested over time and there is also the risk that such technical offices perceive refugees and migrants as groups needing specialised services, with a tendency to develop parallel structures and work in silos. *Other configurations could ensure a more holistic view and better accountability regarding the integration process at the highest level of the city's decision-making structure, while supporting the work of the Social Policies Department.*

- **Co-ordination and evaluation across levels of government**. Despite the existence of legislative frameworks, plans and dialogue mechanisms (see page 32 and 40), effective co-ordination across levels of government with regard to long-term integration issues could be improved. As previous OECD analysis emphasised, a large number of political and institutional bodies charged with co-ordinating and streamlining integration policy exist in Italy. The challenge is to identify which are most likely to deliver concretely and to influence integration investments (OECD, 2014). Efforts to streamline integration policies exist. Still, both the Lazio plan for integration and the social plan identify strengthening governance systems and inter-institutional relations as an objective. For the time being, city and regional plans with an impact on migration issues (i.e. plan to address Roma communities' health issues, etc.) are not always co-ordinated, leading to potential overlap or delivery gaps. *In this sense, some interesting practices for cross-level consultations and evaluation mechanisms can be found in Germany, where integration indicators are formulated by the Conference of the Ministers of Interior of all Länder, together with the federal level; or in the Netherlands, where thematic multi-level and multi-stakeholder consultations are held, for instance, with regard to discrimination in the labour market.*

- **EU funding as a leverage for improving co-ordination among levels of government**. The establishment of the AMIF (Asylum, Migration and Integration Fund of the EU) increased opportunities for close collaboration across levels of government and sectors. The fund is spent by the regions themselves (based on the priorities set by the managing authority for the integration component, i.e. the Ministry of Labour) and merges the European Refugee Fund (ERF) and European Integration Fund (EIF), thus reducing the risk of formulating fragmented policies, where some target economic migrants while others target humanitarian migrants (see page 38). *Within this framework, regions could more systematically establish a dialogue with relevant stakeholders and municipalities to set the local objectives as it has been the case for the Programma Multi-Azione in the Lazio region see page 32.*

- **Collaboration with non-state actors.** Spending restrictions to hiring personnel, difficulties to effectively use public resources; etc. contribute to hinder public actors' capacity to implement integration-related policies and increase their reliance on third-sector actors and service providers (OECD, 2014). This allowed successful integration practices to emerge, more as the result of scattered efforts, rather than through a systematic trajectory. However, given the myriad of stakeholders and external service providers, local authorities often face difficulties assuming control of the direction of local integration policy (Chaloff, 2006). The city started capitalising on this wealth of knowledge, in particular through the SPRAR mechanisms (see page 41). *However, a co-ordination platform involving all relevant actors under municipal guidance, with clear objectives and indicators, as well as more stable funding mechanisms could make collaboration with non-*

state actors more effective. Rome could learn for instance from Barcelona, where NGOs and the municipality co-ordinated provision of services to migrants, in particular regarding language classes.

- **Migrant students' inclusion in public schools.** Stakeholders share the view that in the past it has been easy to enrol children with different backgrounds in Italian public schools at any level, regardless of whether they speak Italian, which is a great advantage for the integration of young newcomers. *However, to maximise their academic success and integration, schools should be supported by appropriate financial and human resources, specifically with trained teachers.*

- **Evaluation of the combined impact of local policies on integration.** In the absence of a clear local strategy for integration, evaluation tools also remain weak. While data on migrant population exist (see page 53), there is no municipal evaluation framework to track results of municipal combined policies to address the gaps this group is experiencing. Despite the absence of an evaluation framework, reports produced on integration by independent local observatories, such as the *Osservatorio Romano sulle Migrazioni*, are used by local authorities for instance in the formulation of the calls for public tenders for outsourcing integration-related services. *It would be helpful to enhance the use of data on migrant outcomes by policy makers to adjust future policy decisions. Evidence-based policy-making mechanisms in Gothenburg and Vienna can serve as examples of using data on social exclusion (e.g. origin, neighbourhood, education, etc.) to formulate more sustainable city policies.*

- **Access the local labour markets.** In a national context, where many labour contracts are informal (Chaloff, 2006), with the informal sector accounting for and estimated 12% of Italian GDP in 2013 and 35% of this underground economy being produced through undeclared work (ISTAT, 2015), migrants as well as nationals do not often rely on public employment services (Centres for Employment CpI, Centre for orientation in the labour market COL, etc.), but rather on informal networks to find a job (see page 54). Some small-scale experiences funded by the municipality were successful in integrating refugees in the formal labour market (see page 56). *Building on the work of existing vocational and employment services, the municipality could play a more active role in matching labour supply and demand in the formal local job market, including to the benefit of migrants. In addition the municipality can play a key role in raising migrants' and employers' awareness of labour rights and improving appeal mechanisms, in collaboration with the unions.*

- **Validation of migrants' competences and education titles.** There seems to be little investment at city level in tools to validate migrant competencies and diplomas. This is understanable in a context, where the demand for skilled jobs is low. However, a lack of perspective to move towards a position that is aligned with the level of migrants' competences and qualifications might negatively impact the motivation of newcomers to fully integrate in Italian society and could be an incentive to move on to another EU country. *Some innovative municipal experiences with regard to competency assessment (Amsterdam, Berlin) and facilitation of qualification validation (Gothenburg) can be of interest to Rome.*

- **Awareness raising on access to health systems.** A complete regional (Lazio) legal framework for migrant health policies (see page 59) has guaranteed a full access to healthcare for regular and irregular migrants. This legal framework of social and health issues made institutions respond with relevant policies and actions, guaranteeing migrants a better quality of life. The third sector played a key role in advocating for migrant health-related issues during the formulation of the legal framework, providing local authorities with important insights on migrants' health issues at local level. In addition to adapted services in the public health systems, 15 clinics in Rome, which are run by the region (ASL), offer services for welcoming migrants as well as a specialised clinic, San Gallicano, which offers integrated care for migrants. Specialised integrated support for victims of violence and torture is provided in SA.MI.FO. (Salute Migranti Forzati - Forced Migrant Health). *However, administrative obstacles to access the national healthcare system persist, and migrants often lack information about their rights to access health services or fear to do so, when they are irregular. Thus, further efforts are still needed to fill the gap between the right to access healthcare and exercising this right.*

Best practices that could be replicated

- **SPRAR, a protection system that encourages multi-level as well as local multi-stakeholder coordination.** The reception system for asylum seekers and refugees – as described from page 41 – is largely managed by NGOs through either a national-local-NGOs co-ordination mechanism (the SPRAR network), or a national-NGOs mechanism without local authorities' involvement (CAS). In Rome, the SPRAR system strengthened horizontal collaboration between the municipality, the third-sector and NGOs with significant expertise in reception of newcomers. It also contributed to improving vertical co-ordination: reception solutions are selected by the municipality according to the capacity and expertise of the local stakeholders, through a transparent process. Management standards, monitoring and funding are guaranteed by the national level. In June 2016, approximately 7 400 asylum seekers and refugees were estimated to be hosted in the Metropolitan City of Rome. Between 2014 and 2016, 55 SPRAR centres existed in the city of Rome (see page 41). Lately, the city has improved the transparency of the selection process and contract management with the entities in charge of the structures following the guidance of the national anti-corruption authority. Since the approval of the Security Decree in November 2018, some provisions of the national reception system have undergone substantial changes, whose implications are not reflected in this case study at the moment of the publication (March 2019) .

- **Innovative housing experience for recognised refugees.** Semi-autonomous homes (see page 47) were built in response to the critical juncture, when recognised refugees leave the reception system (6-12 months after recognition) and have to find their place in society on their own. Some refugees find shelter in the semi-autonomous residencies that several NGOs and faith-based organisations have set up since 2015. Building on their experience in receiving vulnerable migrants, these organisations opened homes, where refugees have to contribute with a monthly fee. Refugees can stay in these houses for six extra months, during which social workers orient them toward municipal and other local services in the process of finding a house and a job. One of the objectives is to create links with the neighbourhood, helping the newcomers build their social capital but also defeating prejudices of local communities and stereotypes about the privileged treatment that refugees receive. Unfortunately, these houses only host a very small number of refugees, while many others end up living in squats and other spontaneous settlements. A more systematic approach to temporary housing could be inspired by the Municipality of Stockholm which has built since 2015 350 modular units to ensure the transition for recognised refugees, until they find a permanent accommodation. During up to five years they can live in modular houses paying a monthly fee.

- **Proactive co-ordination and experience-sharing mechanisms among non-state actors in Rome**, active in integration-related matters. Good examples are the Network *Scuolemigranti* (see page 52) and the "*Comunità di Ospitalità*" (see page 47). These networks establish a direct dialogue with the municipality of Rome that can help them find spaces and sometimes other institutional actors can delegate to them some activities (e.g. collaboration between public schools and Scuolemigranti).

- **Mechanisms to ensure access to services to the most marginalised groups.** To make sure that "marginalised" people (including migrants, refugees and irregular migrants living in spontaneous settlements) can ask for municipal residence registration – and thus access the national health system – the municipality of Rome gives them a fake address in "Via Modesta Valenti", thus providing them with a temporary residence.

Chapter 1. Key data on migrant presence and integration in Rome

This chapter compiles key statistics on the presence and integration outcomes of migrant population in Rome and in comparison to the rest of the country. In 2017 non-EU residents in Rome metropolitan area represented 9.3% of total non-EU residents in Italy while in the city of Rome foreign residents represents 13% of total population, concentrated in certain districts. Initially migration to Italy consisted of low-skilled migrants and is more recently characterised by family reunification and a growing number of native-born offspring of immigrants. The chapter also provides an insight on the national migration legislative framework.

Box 1.1. Definition of migrant and refugee

The term "migrant" generally functions as an umbrella term used to describe people that move to another country with the intention of staying for a significant period of time. According to the United Nations (UN), a long-term migrant is "a person who moves to a country other than that of his or her usual residence for a period of at least a year (12 months)" (UNSD, 2017). Yet, not all migrants move for the same reasons, have the same needs or are subject to the same laws.

This report considers migrants a large group that includes:

- •Persons who have emigrated to an EU country from another EU country ('EU migrants'),
- •Persons who have come to an EU country from a non-EU country ('non-EU born or third-country national'),
- •Native-born children of immigrants (often referred to as the 'second generation'), and
- •Persons who have fled their country of origin and are seeking/ have obtained international protection.

For the latter, some distinctions are needed. While asylum seekers and refugees are often counted as a subset of migrants and included in official estimates of migrant stocks and flows, this is not correct according to the UN's definition that indicates that "migrant" does not refer to refugees, displaced, or others forced or compelled to leave their homes:

"The term 'migrant' in Article 1.1 (a) should be understood as covering all cases where the decision to migrate is taken freely by the individual concerned, for reasons of 'personal convenience' and without the intervention of an external compelling factor" (IOM Constitution Article 1.1 (a)).

According to recent OECD work the term "migrant" is a generic term for anyone moving to another country with the intention of staying for a certain period of time – not, in other words, tourists or business visitors. It includes both permanent and temporary migrants with a valid residence permit or visa, asylum seekers, and undocumented migrants who do not belong to any of the three groups (OECD, 2016b).

Thus, in this report the following terms are used:

- •"Status holder" or "refugee" who have successfully applied for asylum and have been granted some sort of protection in their host country, including those who are recognised on the basis of the 1951 Geneva Convention Relating to the Status of Refugees, but also those benefiting from national asylum laws or EU legislation (Directive 2011/95/EU), such as the subsidiary protection status. This corresponds to the category 'humanitarian migrants' meaning recipients of protection – be it refugee status, subsidiarity or temporary protection – as used in recent OECD work (OECD, 2016b).
- •'Asylum seeker' for those individuals who have submitted a claim for international protection but are awaiting the final decision.

- • 'Rejected asylum seeker' for those individuals who have been denied protection status.
- • 'Undocumented or irregular migrants' for those who do not have a legal permission to stay.

This report systematically distinguishes which group is targeted by policies and services put in place by the city. Where statistics provided by the cities included refugees in the migrant stocks and flows, it will be indicated accordingly.

The Statistical Unit of Roma Capitale (City of Rome) and ISTAT (Italian Statistical Authority) consider in their statistics the category Foreign Resident (Straniero dimorante abitualmente) to refer to persons with non-Italian citizenship (excluding persons who have dual citizenship, i.e. both Italian and non-Italian citizenship who count as Italians) who regularly reside in their accommodation or cohabitate, and who have a residence permit to stay in Italy (work permit, family reunification permit, or request of first or renewal of residence permit)[1]

Key Statistics

Figure 1.1. Cittá Metropolitana di Roma Capitale (equivalent to the TL3 area)

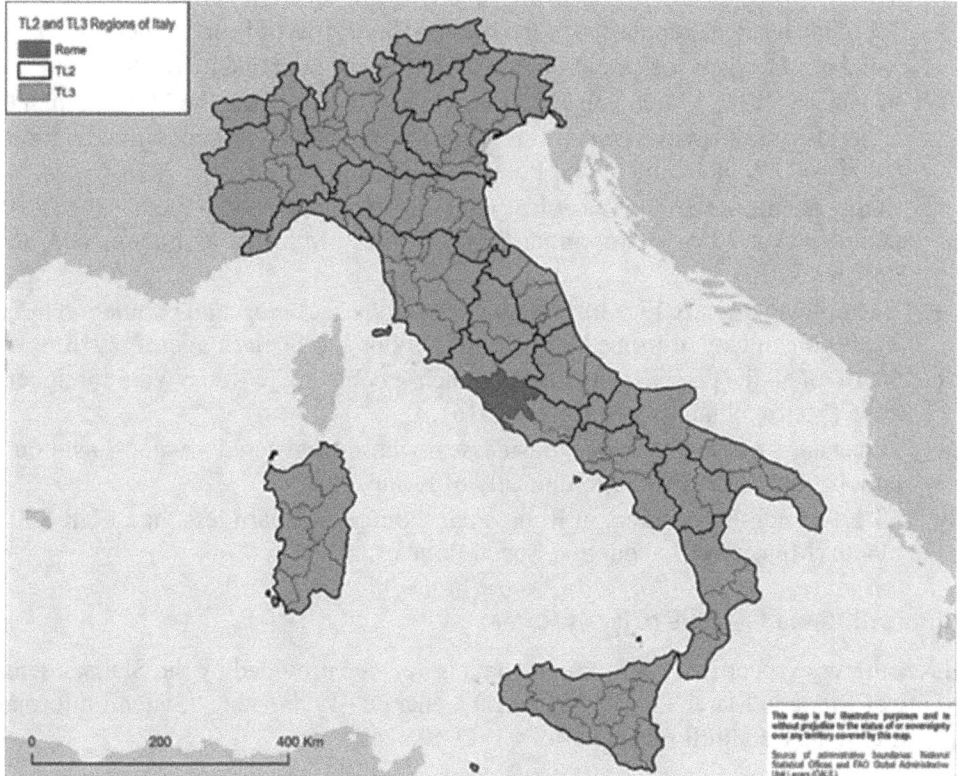

Note: Territorial Level 2 (TL2) consists of the OECD classification of regions within each member country. There are 335 regions classified at this level across 35-member countries. Territorial Level 3 (TL3) consists of the lower level of classification and is composed of 1681 small regions. In most cases, they correspond to administrative regions. *Source*: OECD (2018), OECD Regional Statistics Database, http://dx.doi.org/10.1787/region-data-en.

Municipality	TL3	TL2	State
Rome	Città Metropolitana di Roma Capitale	Lazio Region	Italy

National level

Total resident population; 60 589 445 (1 January 2017, ISTAT[2])

Foreign resident population: 5 047 028 (1 January 2017, ISTAT[3])

In 2017, the presence of irregular migrants represented 8.2% of the total foreign population (ISMU, 2017)

- Country subnational government expenditure as a % of GDP: 28.7% vs. OECD34 average of 40.2%

Città Metropolitana di Roma Capitale – Metropolitan City of Rome – ex Provincia di Roma – is composed of 121 municipalities – The Mayor of the metropolitan area is also the mayor of the City of Rome.

- Population of the Metropolitan City: 4.3 million
- Foreigner residents on 1 January 2017: 544 956 persons[4]
- Non-EU foreign residents: 345 897 as of January 2017, this represents 9.3% of total non-EU residents in Italy (Minister of labour and social policies, 2018)
- 7% of the resident population of the Metropolitan Area of Rome are non-EU citizen
- Number of asylum seekers: 4 063 in 2016 in Metropolitan City of Rome.
- In January 2016, 15 006 non-EU citizens were registered in the Metropolitan City either as either asylum seekers, refugees or subsidiary protection status holders (Ministry of Labour and Social Policies, 2016)
- Employment rate 15-64 year-olds: 66% for immigrant population; 61% for total population in 2015 Metropolitan City of Rome (Ministry of Labour and Social Policies, 2016)
- Unemployment rate: 13% for migrant population; 11% for total population in 2014 Metropolitan City of Rome (Ministry of Labour and Social Policies, 2016)
- 10.7% of all the persons who declared their income tax in Rome were foreigners in 2015 (Metropolitan City of Rome, 2016)
- Percentage of single-owner businesses whose registered owner has non-EU nationality: 18.7% (Metropolitan City of Rome, 2016
- 53.2% of non-EU workers in Rome metropolitan area earn less than EUR 800 per month (Ministry of Labour and Social Policies, 2016)

Comune di Roma Capitale (City of Rome)

Unless otherwise specified, the following data have been provided by the Statistic Unit of the City of Rome in March 2017 (Ragioneria Generale - I Direzione "Sistemi informativi di pianificazione e controllo finanziario" - U.O. Statistica).

- Roma Capitale - Comune di Roma: composed of 15 districts (Municipi)
- Total city population: 2 864 731 (2016)
- 377 217 foreign residents in the City of Rome as of January 2017 (Roma Capitale, 2017)
- Foreign residents represent 13.1% of the total residents in Rome

- 70% of the foreign-born population living in the Roma Metropolitan area are registered in the City of Rome (Comune di Roma)
- Number of unaccompanied minors 340 in 2016 in Metropolitan City of Rome
- The most important countries of origin: Romania, Philippines, Bangladesh, China.
- Educational Attainment (Primary; Secondary; High School, University) – % for foreign residents; % for all resident population
    - Primary: 34.9% of migrant population; 10.9% of all resident population achieved primary level
    - Secondary: 20.3% of migrant population, 10.8% of all resident population achieved secondary education
    - High School: 26.3% of migrant population; 8.5% of all resident population achieved high school level.
    - University: 18.7% of migrant population

Migration flows

National level

In Italy the foreign-born population has multiplied by fourteen between 1990 and 2015, from 356 159 in 1991 to about five million in 2015 (OECD, 2017) accounting for 10% of the working-age population in 2011/12 (OECD, 2014). Around one third of foreign residents originate from EU and 3 714 136 (2017) are non-EU regular migrants (ISTAT, 2018). According to Eurostat, Italy is now the fifth country of the European Union in terms of the size of the immigrant population and the first country for acquisition of citizenship.

Total residence permits issued to foreigners decreased from 600 000 permits issued in 2010 to 226 934 in 2017. However the share of international protection permits, among total permits increased from 7.5% in 2010 to 34.5% that were granted during 2016[5]. After a decree was issued in 2017 (see page 21), a quota of labour permits was set up that is equal to 30 850 permits, which was on par with the previous year, 18 000 of which were reserved to entries for seasonal work and a big part for converting residence permits such as student permits (Ministry of Labour and Social Policies, 2017).

In 2016, arrivals at the Italian shores reached 180 000 people and 120 000 asylum applications were registered (OECD, 2017).

Initially, migration to Italy consisted mainly of low-skilled migrants; however, more recently family reunification has led to a large settled immigrant population and a growing number of native-born offspring of immigrants (OECD, 2014).

A signal of the stabilisation of immigrant population is the increase of the number of individuals who acquired Italian citizenship. In 2015 the number was 178 035 (ISTAT, 2018), which was a 21% increase compared to 2014; and in 2016, 185 000 non-EU residents obtained citizenship, 40% of them were under 20 years old (Ministry of Labour and Social policies, 2018). It is estimated that approximately 1 million foreign residents between 16 and 18 years of age would be naturalised if the law on nationality (see page 21) would pass. Some immigrants leave the country once they receive Italian citizenship. In 2016, 28 000 foreign-born persons who obtained Italian citizenship emigrated (+19% compared to 2015), 50% of them returned to the country of origin, 43% move to another EU country and 7% to another non-EU country (ISTAT, 2017).

The Metropolitan area of Rome

Rome is the second metropolitan city in Italy in terms of non-EU residents after Milan. The presence of non-EU residents increased in the Metropolitan area of Rome by 37% between 2011 and 2017 while it increased by 5% at national level (Ministry of Labour and Social policies, 2018). Compared to other Italian metropolises, foreign residents in Rome seem less stable: 50% of non-EU migrants have a long-term resident permit (lungo soggiornanti) compared to 70% in Venice and 61% in Genova and the national average being 60% (Ministry of Labour and Social policies, 2018).

The City of Rome

Table 1.1. Foreign residents in the City of Rome (Roma Capitale)

Population	Native population	Foreign resident population	Foreign resident from the EU	Other European foreign residents	Non-European foreign residents	Total population
Number of people	2 499 550	377 217**	181 781***	66 359***	107 620***	2 864 731*

Source: *Istat (2015); ** Roma Capitale (2017); *** Centro Studi e Ricerche IDOS (2016a).

In 2016 44.3%of foreigners () resident in the City of Rome came from Europe the second biggest community of foreign residents originated from Asia (33.3%), followed by Africa (12.0%) and the Americas (10.3%) (Roma Capitale, 2017).

In fact, the top five nationalities of foreign residents in Rome are from a European or Asian country, with 24% of foreigners coming from Romania, followed by three Asian countries, respectively Philippines (11%), Bangladesh (8%) and China (5%). The fifth is Ukraine representing 4% of foreigners.

Foreign distribution across Municipal districts in Rome is diversified. In Municipio (district) I, foreigners represent 24% of the total population whereas in Municipio IX they account for 8.2% (Metropolitan City of Rome, 2016).

Figure 1.2. Percentage of foreign population over total population per district, 2015

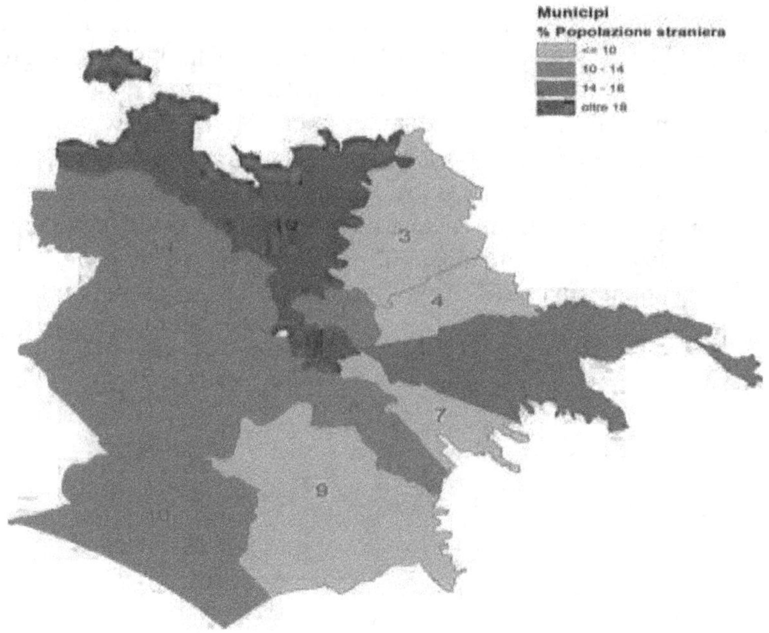

Note: The highest concentration of migrant is registered in Municipio I (24.1%, 45 014 foreign residents in 2015); Municipio VI (17%, 43 377 residents in 2015) and Municipio V (15.8%, 39 000 residents in 2015) (Metropolitan City of Rome, 2016).
Source: Anagrafe Roma.

Migration legal framework (See page 75)

In the past the Government regulated migratory flows mainly through the annual flows decree 'Decreti Flussi'. It checked annually the labour need of the territory, and it established the number of foreigners who could enter the country for work reasons. The Government has often – though not always – been able to manage the flows in advance, and regularisation programmes (Sanatorie) have allowed irregular migrants present in Italy to obtain residence permits. Eight regularisation programmes took place between 1980 and 2012 and a new one was announced for 2018[6]. In 2002, the largest regularisation programme saw around 700 000 applications received, a large share of applications was for domestic work and caregiving, reflecting both the change in the labour market for immigrants and the more favourable eligibility criteria (OECD, 2014). Since 2002, the Bossi-Fini law distinguishes between "clandestine" migrants, that is to say foreigners entering Italy without a regular visa and "irregular" migrants, foreigners who no longer meet residence requirements (permit). According to current legislation, clandestine immigrants are punishable by a fine or detention or by expulsion.

Since 2012[7] the Integration Agreement (see page 24) came into action and made learning Italian a requirement for obtaining a residence permit exceeding one year for non-EU citizens (excluding international protection applicants, or migrants citing family reasons).

The condition for obtaining Italian citizenship through naturalisation is ongoing, documented residence in Italy for ten years and it depends on the decision of the public administration. The foreigner who is born in Italy, and who resides there for 18 years without any interruption, in order to acquire Italian citizenship, has to declare the willingness to acquire it before his or her 19th birthday. In 2017, a proposal based on the 'Ius-soli' principle was discussed in the Parliament to reduce the delay for acquiring citizenship for children of regular migrants born in Italy. The law would give access to citizenship after 16 years of residence for individuals who have done their schooling in Italy. The law has been discussed several times since 1992 and was again rejected in December 2017. Family reunification is granted to all migrants who have a regular permit for work (for at least one year), asylum, subsidiary protection, study, religion, family, long-term stay, or pending naturalisation. There are two requisites to fulfil: having a minimum income, and an adequate accommodation. Beneficiaries of refugee or subsidiarity protection status do not have to fulfil such criteria.

Notes

[1] Glossario ISTAT, https://www.istat.it/it/metodi-e-strumenti/glossario.

[2] http://dati.istat.it/Index.aspx?DataSetCode=DCIS_POPRES1.

[3] http://dati.istat.it/Index.aspx?DataSetCode=DCIS_POPRES1.

[4] http://dati.istat.it/Index.aspx?DataSetCode=DCIS_POPRES1.

[5] www.integrazionemigranti.gov.it/Attualita/Approfondimenti/Pagine/Le-comunita-migranti-in-Italia--Dati-al-primo-gennaio-2017.aspx.

[6] https://www.diritto.it/la-regolarizzazione-degli-stranieri-italia/.

[7] Decreto ministeriale del 4/6/2010, Decreto del Presidente della Repubblica 14 settembre 2011, n. 179.

Chapter 2. The Checklist for public action to migrant integration at the local level applied to the city of Rome

*Chapter 1 gives a description of the actions, policy framework and governance mechanisms for migrants and refugees inclusion in Rome. The chapter is structured following the **Checklist for public action to migrant integration at the local level**, as included in the Synthesis Report **"Working Together for Local Integration of Migrants and Refugees"** (OECD, 2018). The checklist comprises a list of 12 key evidence-based objectives that can be used by policy makers and practitioners in the development and implementation of migrant integration programmes, at local, regional, national and international levels. This checklist highlights for the first-time a common framework to describe a holistic territorial approach to inclusion across contexts that have very different institutional and socio-economic characteristics.*

This innovative tool has been elaborated by the OECD as part of the larger study on supported by the European Commission, Directorate General for regional and urban policies. Chapter 2.

> **Box 2.1. A checklist for public action to migrant integration at the local level**
>
> **Block 1. Multi-level governance: Institutional and financial settings**
>
> Objective 1. Enhance effectiveness of migrant integration policy through improved vertical co-ordination and implementation at the relevant scale.
>
> Objective 2. Seek policy coherence in addressing the multi-dimensional needs of, and opportunities for, migrants at the local level.
>
> Objective 3. Ensure access to, and effective use of, financial resources that are adapted to local responsibilities for migrant integration.
>
> **Block 2. Time and space: Keys for migrants and host communities to live together**
>
> Objective 4. Design integration policies that take time into account throughout migrants' lifetimes and evolution of residency status.
>
> Objective 5. Create spaces where the interaction brings migrant and native-born communities closer
>
> **Block 3. Local capacity for policy formulation and implementation**
>
> Objective 6. Build capacity and diversity in civil service, with a view to ensure access to mainstream services for migrants and newcomers
>
> Objective 7. Strengthen co-operation with non-state stakeholders, including through transparent and effective contracts.
>
> Objective 8. Intensify the assessment of integration results for migrants and host communities and their use for evidence-based policies.
>
> **Block 4. Sectoral policies related to integration**
>
> Objective 9. Match migrant skills with economic and job opportunities.
>
> Objective 10. Secure access to adequate housing.
>
> Objective 11. Provide social welfare measures that are aligned with migrant inclusion.
>
> Objective 12. Establish education responses to address segregation and provide equitable paths to professional growth.

Block 1: Multi-level governance: Institutional and financial settings

Objective 1: Enhance effectiveness of migrant integration policy through vertical co-ordination and implementation at the relevant scale

National and local visions of integration

"Governance of integration" appeared in Italy only in the late 1980s. Relatively late appearance of migration inflows, and incredibly rapid growth, are among the causes of a delayed institutional integration response that is still characterised by small-scale and time–limited projects (OECD, 2014).

Yet migrants benefit from access to almost all public services, civil rights (right to a legal defence, antidiscrimination, etc.) and social rights such as family reunification, health (granted also to irregular migrants) and education on the same basis as Italian citizens. In terms of political rights, non-EU migrants do not have the right to participate in local elections as opposed to EU citizens – as is the case in most of the other countries examined in this study. Historically, voluntary and third sector organisations (especially faith-based ones), migrant associations, social partners (trade, business associations and unions) have played a key role in local and national systems for migrant integration, and generated a myriad of solutions adapting rapidly to changing local needs. Thus, the first characteristic of an integration vision at all levels is to be a multi-stakeholder.

The conceptual framework of integration in Italy varied across time. The discourse moved from an universal approach towards migrants - the need to ensure equal rights to everyone - to an emphasis on diversity - ensuring the right to cultural belonging, while avoiding both assimilation and ghettoization, to a need for integration based on utility ("wanted but not welcomed", following a well-known phrase of Zolberg, 1987) and a security discourse (at the local level, but also in terms of border control). These oscillations are well reflected in the successive laws with regards migration and asylum summarised in Annex B. In particular, in 1998 the Turco-Napolitano law (Testo unico sull'immigrazione –TUI-) understood integration mainly as employment: integration in the labour market was a necessary and sufficient condition when accompanied by the right of access to public services (OECD, 2014). The law also established a national fund for immigrants' integration – then merged in 2002 with social policies fund – and gives to local administrations (regions, municipalities) crucial roles for immigrants' integration. Finally it created the Territorial Councils for Immigration (CTI) and the National Co-ordinating body (ONC) in the National Council for Economy and Labour (CNEL).

The current national strategy the "*Plan for integration in security - identity and encounter*" signed by the Ministry of Labour and Social Policy, Ministry of Interior and Ministry of Education was formulated in 2010[1]. The model identifies five priority areas: education from language to values, employment, housing and space management, access to basic services, minors and second generation, instruments for integration in particular by facilitating access to information and coherent governance of integration policies. According to the analysis of the CNEL, this policy has a flaw: failure to recognise obstacles to integration as structural weaknesses of broader social policies, which also affects Italian citizens. The analysis suggests seeing integration priorities as opportunities to reform Italian societal structure. For instance with regards to housing, targeted policies for migrants fail to recognise that access to housing is an emergency for a growing percentage of the Italian population (CNEL, 2010).

In contrast more recent documents drafted by sub-national governments are geared towards strengthening the quality of overall public services, to better respond to the needs of vulnerable groups including migrants. This approach is in line with the responses adopted in most EU countries analysed through this study. For instance, the 2015 EU-funded integration project (see paragraph below on the Lazio Region), implemented in the Region Lazio, describes integration measures in Lazio as contributing at increasing the overall quality of territorial services. "The project aims at requalifying territorial services, from a systemic point of view, for better service delivery to immigrant, refugee and, in general, vulnerable users" ("il progetto si pone come obiettivo la riqualificazione dei servizi territoriali, in un'ottica sistemica, per una migliore risposta all'utenza immigrata, rifugiata e, in generale, vulnerabile") (Region of Lazio, 2016).

With regard to integration measures targeting persons benefitting from international protection, the Government developed in 2017 a National integration Plan for refugees (see page 41). This document is the result of a National Co-ordination Work Group established within the Department for Civil Liberties and Immigration of the Ministry of Interior.

National-level integration measures

As mentioned in section 1.3 since 2012 all applicants for long-term residence permits (longer than one year) have to sign the Integration Agreement with the Italian State. Migrants commit to acquire within two years A2 level knowledge of Italian and of civic principles, fulfil obligations with regards to the education and fiscal contributions. In addition, the long-term residence permit (EC residence permit obtained after five years of residence) is conditional on passing a language test. As part of this contract, the State guarantees fundamental civil rights, access to work, health and education and favour the integration process "through the adoption of any suitable initiative, in connection with Regional Governments, Local Authorities and non-profit associations"[2]. Language training is the only targeted national integration measure provided mainly through the Provincial centres for adult education (CPIAs) managed by the Ministry of Education (see section 2.4.4). However, as previously observed (OECD, 2014) the offer of language classes is low in terms of hours provided (100 as compared to well above 300 in other OECD countries) and the language level target is rather low, with no vocational-specific courses.

In recent years, regulations and jurisprudence are evolving towards improved migrants' access to social rights. For instance, when it comes to self-certification, foreigners do not benefit from the same rights as Italians. Migrants still have to produce certification to prove, for example, their family relationships, family unit, eligibility for accommodation, etc. These documents are needed for the issue and renewal of a residence permit. A full equalisation between these two categories has been postponed by the budget law five times since 2013 (Ministry of Labour and Social Policies, 2017). Furthermore, an appeal of the Court of Milan in December 2017 ruled illegal a circular from INPS (National Institute of Social Security) limiting the access to a EUR 800 Childbirth Bonus only to Italian mothers and immigrant mothers with a long-term resident permit. This ruling extends the right to the bonus to all mothers legally present in Italy (Ministry of Labour and Social Policies, 2017).

National actors involved in integration-relevant policies

All the countries analysed through this study face challenges in coordinating the actors involved in establishing a systematic integration policies. The challenge "to make policies for integration integrated" starts from the national level and has an impact across sub-national levels. Many countries experiment solutions to mainstream integration questions across all relevant line ministries.

The trend in recent year has been towards dismantling national ministries for migration and integration (Greece being the exception across the nine EU countries examined as the Ministry for Migration policy was set up in 2016) and to use other tools and dialogue mechanisms to implement the national integration objectives across line ministries. For instance since 1978 Germany has established a Commissioner for Immigration, Refugees and Integration who acts as a ministry position within the Federal government. Its role is to advise the government, working across all ministries involved in migration-relevant policies, rather than act as a multi-level co-ordinator. It has the lead on designing the federal integration strategy and co-ordinates and evaluates the National Integration and Action Plan (OECD, 2018[1]).

In Italy this report identified two main tools for inter-ministerial coordination, one is to mainstream efforts for migrants integration across ministries (the 2010 "Plan of integration in security - identity and encounter" signed by the Ministry of Labour, interior and education) and more recently the efforts for mainstreaming refugee integration across sectors by establishing the National Co-ordination work group involving Ministry of the Interior and Ministry of Labour in charge of formulating the *2017 National Refugee Integration Plan*. However for these tools to ensure consistency in policy action on the ground, they could be associated to concrete targets in the budget of each Ministry involved in their implementation and with operational evaluation frameworks.

The following paragraph lists the Italian national institutions that are involved in integration policies:

The UNAR (National office against racial discrimination) is body within the Department for equal opportunities of the Presidency of the Council of Ministers, which works for the promotion of equal treatment and the elimination of ethnic and racial discrimination. The department acts as a reference point for the victims of racial and ethnic discrimination, and monitors the effectiveness of instruments aimed at equality of treatment between persons. It works in co-operation with trade unions and business associations to promote positive action through training courses, information campaigns and the promotion of codes of conduct in the workplace.

The Ministry of Education (MIUR) provides free adult language training within the framework of the general system of adult education through the so-called *Centri Provinciali d'Istruzione per Adulti* Provincial Adults Education Center (CPIA), known before as Centri Territoriali Permanenti CTP. For these courses the Ministry uses the existing personnel of the public school system, provides guidelines, curricular and limited financial support. Schools have at the same time a wide organisational autonomy.

Another key actor at national level is the Directorate General for Immigration and of Integration policy within the Ministry of Labour and Social Policy (MLPS), which has the following main tasks:

- Migration policy: it participates in the annual planning procedures of migration flows
- Formulation of Integration Policy: it co-ordinates the policies for social and labour integration of migrants, defining the overall framework for integration. The current overall framework for integration of was defined in 2010 by the "*Plan of integration in security - identity and encounter*".
- Multi-level integrated programming: the ministry signs with the Regions the Accordi di Programma (Programme agreements) defining joint objectives in terms of labour market integration (see paragraph below on the Lazio region). Several stakeholders questioned the effectiveness of these agreements in translating into actions on the ground.
- Integration Financing: it manages the national resources for integration policy (see page 38) and it has the delegation from the Minister of the Interior as managing authority for the Integration component of the Asylum Migration and Integration Fund (AMIF) Fund

- Integration Evaluation: it produces annual reports on migrant integration in the labour market, integration in Italian metropolitan cities and integration of migrant per national communities in Italy[3] (see page 53).
- Information on Integration policies: since 2012 it manages a website (integrazionemigranti.gov.it) to facilitate access to integration services. The website is the result of collaboration with the Ministry of Interior and Education. Besides gathering all recent publication and research on integration, the website provides information for migrants with regard to housing, work, language classes, intercultural mediation, health and under-aged migrants. This website also maps migrant associations registered in the Italian territory, as of 2016 there were 2 118 registered in the database[4] as well as service providers listed for each area of integration identified in the national Strategy (language, employment, housing, essential services and minors and second generation). The portal is meant as a single institutional information source for migrants as well as employers and all public and private actors involved in the field of integration policies.

The Ministry of Interior, through a series of offices among which the Department for civil rights and immigration has the following tasks:

- National migration policy definition: it participates in the annual planning procedures of migration flows
- Integration Policy implementation: it co-ordinates the Sportelli Unici per l'Immigrazione(Art. 22 L. 189 of 2000) and the Consigli Territoriali per l'Immigrazione (Art. 3 D. Lgs. 286/1998) which work as co-ordination entities between the national and the local level.
- Financing: manage European funds for migration as the AMIF
- Asylum policy implementation: the Ministry funds and plans the reception system (CIE, CARA, CAS, SPRAR) which are then managed at lower levels through the Prefectures and NGOs (see page 41).

The Ministry of Interior is present in the local territory through two main bodies: Prefectures and Police Headquarters.

The Ministry of the Interior is responsible for issuing migrants' residence permits. The bureaucratic procedures (i.e. work permits, family reunification, obtaining the residence permit, etc.) are managed at the provincial level at the *Sportelli Unici per l'Immigrazione* (Single Immigration Desks) within the Prefectures. These offices release the authorisation for subordinate and seasonal jobs of non-EU citizens within the quotas established by the annual flows decree or for the conversion (for example from study to work permit or from seasonal to subordinate work). These offices also manage the practices for the implementation of the integration agreement. For instance, migrants can apply here for the language test. These desks are supposed to represent different bodies responsible for integration (such as the Ministry of Interior, Ministry of Labour, tax agencies, etc.) in the territory (OECD, 2014). In practice, the Single Immigration Desks essentially cover matters of entry (issuance and renewal of work permit, entry of family members) and do not deal with enrolment in the health system, school system, or municipal residence procedures, etc.

The CNEL (*Conisglio nazionale dell'economia e del lavoro* – National economic council) is an organ composed of representatives of the government and social partners (chamber of commerce, union, etc.) which has competence on economic and social legislation. Within this body, the ONC (Organismo Nazionale di coordinamento per le politiche di integrazione degli stranieri) is composed of migrant representatives of social partners (unions and chambers of commerce, etc.) as well as NGO representatives, experts of the sector and the CNEL members. It is mandated to increase the participation of immigrants in "public life", and to circulate information.

Lazio Region

Regions lead integration activities, establishing objectives in their areas of competence including labour, vocational training, housing, social welfare and health. As these sectors pertain to either joint regulations between central government and regions or to the residual regulations of the regions, the central government cannot set up objectives or initiate activities pre-defined at the central level (OECD, 2014). For instance, health is a "concurrent" legislative area, meaning the national level establishes the standards (Livelli essenziali di Assistenza – Essential levels of Assistance) and the regions are in charge of implementing them. Social policies are exclusive regional competence (Art 117, 2001 Constitutional reform)[5].

The Turco-Napolitano Law of 1998 (286/1998) assigned to regions more competences with regard to migrant integration and established that the resources of regional social policies would co-finance integration. The national integration system is supported by specific *regional integration laws*, which regulate the actions to be planned and implemented within their territory in the field of social integration. On this point Italian regions are forerunners in developing territorial, cross-sectoral legislative frameworks for integration. Very few of the other European countries analysed in this study have regional integration laws and most developed them later. For instance in Germany the first Land to develop a regional integration law was the Berlin Land which developed it in 2010. On the contrary, in other European contexts such as in Austria, the first actor who developed integration strategies have been cities (Vienna). Regional laws in Italy are supposed to support the national framework for integration; however, there are no national indicators or reviews that ensure alignment of the regional legislations to the national framework. The Accordi di programma (Programmatic Agreements) described below between the Ministry of labour and social policy and the regions are supposed to be the 'hook' between the two level, but as mentioned their effectiveness of this agreements in translating into action on the ground is debated.

Lazio is one of the Italian regions with a specific and recent integration law the LR.10 / 2008. The regional law shows innovative aspects (Fioretti et al., 2014) also mirrored in its title: *Regulations for the promotion and protection of the exercise of civil and social rights and the full equality of foreign immigrant citizens*. The law is a multi-dimensional integration framework - work, housing, participation, etc. - promoting "the removal of obstacles that hinder the exercise of civil and social rights by immigrant foreign nationals, in order to ensure them conditions equal to those of Italian citizens" (Art.1.1 of the Law). However, some of the most innovative aspects of the law (for example the establishment of a regional board for immigration) have never been implemented.

The law clearly outlines the tasks of the Region, Provinces and Municipalities. In particular, the Region has the following tasks: planning, regulation and direct implementation of the interventions considered of particular interest, as well as of monitoring, control and evaluation.

The main departments within Lazio Region with a mandate related to integration are the Health Department, the Labour Department, the Training department and the Social Policy Department.

The Social Policy Direction and in particular the Department Reception and Inclusion promotes targeted as well as generic initiatives with an impact on migrant integration. In fact, this department is in charge of the integrated territorial system of social and health services (Distretti Socio-Sanitari) of which migrants and nationals are users. The guidelines for the entire regional system of social policies are set in the "Regional Social Plan 2017-2019". The overall social investments for the next three years are around EUR 583 million. Promoting the reception and integration of the "new citizens" is one of the key targets of this policy document and it is spelled out as: monitoring the migration flows, upgrading the reception system, supporting social and labour integration, especially through language tuition, fighting discrimination, strengthening the integration governance system and inter-institutional relations. This document should be instrumental also for improving vertical relations between the regional and municipal social services and in view of addressing overlaps in service provision. However, there seems to be room for improving the co-ordination with the municipal "Social Governance Plan", which sets the priorities and operational implementation of the city's social services as overlaps seems to persists. For instance from the evidence collected it emerged that both the municipal and regional level had drafted a strategy to address roma health without consulting.

The Labour department is in charge of professional training. The ministry of Labour and Social Affairs is in charge of setting up performance levels and the regions are in charge of planning, organising and providing VET either through public tenders (e.g. private associations, enterprises, etc.) or directly, through public vocational training centres (OECD, 2014). The Minister of Labour recognises the regional level as the most strategic for designing and implementing integration policies given their competences on key policy sectors such as professional training, social and health policies. In recent years it increased the cooperation with the Labour departments of regions through calls for proposals and programmatic agreements some specific actions and governance mechanisms targeting migrant labour integration (see section below on multi-level coordination mechanisms).

Finally the Region Lazio also promoted some direct projects aiming at migrant integration with regional funding, in particular the most recent are:

- PRIR Lazio - qualified reception and job placement of refugees
- Italian language courses
- Anti-discrimination Protocol (Agreement with UNAR)
- PRILS LAZIO - Regional Plans for Linguistic and Social Integration of Foreigners in Lazio (see page 62)

The intermediate and municipal level

Regional Law 10/2008 sets a preeminent role for provinces and municipalities in the inclusion of migrants. In particular, the law establishes that provinces promote job orientation and vocational training (through the Job Centres - Centri per l'impiego CPI), education, literacy and language course. The provinces were in charge of the Centri Servizi per l'Immigrazione (Immigration Services Centres) orientation desks, linked to the Centres for Employment offering services of cultural mediation. The role of provinces has been scaled down through successive reforms since 2011. In particular, the provinces are no longer in charge of the definition and implementation of projects within the socio-health districts (piani di zona).

Moreover, the metropolitan city was put in place in 2014 (L. 56/2014, known as "Del Rio law"). Today, the Province of Rome became Metropolitan City of Rome, but with the failure of the referendum for the constitutional law in December 2017, the role of provinces remains uncertain. Within the metropolitan government the main departments involved in migrant integration are: the School and Education Department, the Social Development and Integration Department, the Training and Labour Department[6].

Municipalities in Italy are responsible for the provision of local public services such as pre-school and primary education, and housing (for a more detailed description of the role of the City of Rome; see page 36).

Allocation of competences across levels for integration-related matters

Italian migration policy concerning the management of incoming flows, the control of borders, and the definition of the conditions for staying and expulsion is managed at the national level.

Integration policy that includes all interventions aimed at guaranteeing the civil, social and political rights of regular immigrants (e.g. access to social services and welfare, work, citizenship and political participation, etc) is shared between the national, the regional and the local level. For instance, access to welfare, health and housing is managed at the local level, and is ensured by regions and local authorities.

Access to certain rights – civil, social and even political – is acquired by regular migrants through residence in a municipality (municipal residence registration). Some authors speak about *"policy of residence"* (Gargiulo, 2013): local authorities can regulate access to some local welfare measures for their residents. For instance, concerning public housing, the national law on migrant integration establishes that all migrants having a regular residence permit of at least two years, and a regular job, can access public housing under the same condition as Italians (art. 40, comma 6, d.lgs.286/1998). However, at the regional and local level, norms with a different content have been issued, in the majority of cases adding further length of stay in the territory before accessing social housing.

While the reception policies for asylum seekers and refugees –as will be described in page 41- are largely implemented by NGOs through either a national-local-NGO co-ordination mechanism (the SPRAR network), or a direct national-NGO mechanism; integration policies are mostly outsourced to the third sector by the Regions, the municipality and the social plans (*piani di zona*) or are directly activated through European funds.

This study and previosu OECD work (OECD, 2014) observed that tools for coordination across levels of government exist (see page 32) in Italy, the challenge is to identify which are most likely to deliver concretely and to influence integration investments. Today different national and local integration visions and capacities cohexist across levels of government and across regions. Examples of multi-level governance of integration policies can be considered to reduce risks of fragmentation and heterogeneity in service delivery. A well documented practice is to put in place updated and measurable National Action Plan for integration create instruments to render the results of the integration policy measurable, and associate investments to quantitative indicators. For instance, in Germany the institutionalised dialogue conference of ministers for the integration of the Länder (Integrationsministerministerkonferenz, IntMK) is an interface between the federal level and the Lander. This conference develops indicators that are compared every year across Länder. In the Netherlands the relevant ministers (Labour, etc) organises thematic taskforce on specific migration-related topics (i.e. discrimination in the labour market,etc) involving the four largest municipalities and the associations of municipality, as well as relevant line ministries, in order to design measures that are adapted to local realities. Equally the experts from municipal integration departments (i.e from the City of Amsterdam) have been consulted by the Ministry of the Interior to provide their advice on the new Integration Contract and language class delivery that will be implemented as of 2020. In France the creation in 2018 of the Inter-ministerial Integration Committee and the Inter-ministerial Delegate for Refugee Reception and Integration attests to a shift in integration policy. The shift is both horizontal, setting up a cross-sectoral committee at national level for the formulation of the National Strategy for Refugee Integration (2018-2020), well as vertical as the strategy envisages also local steering committees that will involve *Préfets* and local authorities.

Multi-level co-ordination mechanisms/initatives relevant for integration

The paragraph below lists some of the existing tools for co-ordination and evaluation across levels in place in Italy.

The Consigli Territoriali per l'Immigrazione CTI (Territorial Councils for Immigration) are composed by public - state administration, regions and local governments- and private actors - chamber of commerce, NGOs, organisations working for migrant inclusion and representatives of non-EU employers and employees. Since 1999, CTI are chaired by the Prefect and are present in all Prefectures (DPR 31 8 1999 n. 394). Representatives of CTI report to the Department for Civil Freedom and Migration of the Ministry of Interior, which manages the network ensuring communication and coherence of interventions regarding migrants (Ministry of Interior, 2017).

Since 1999, these bodies monitor the presences of migrant citizens on the territory and local capacity to address their needs.

Main tasks are:

- To gather the local needs connected with migration;
- To promote co-operation in order to favour solutions shared among all institutions and social actors involved for the management of the migratory issue at local level;
- To promote participation of migrant NGOs and organisations representing the migrant community in Italy;
- Bottom-up information mechanisms to inform the central government level, about the interventions and proposals enacted at a provincial level.

They intervene in different areas: e.g. Italian courses, civic courses, provision of services for children born of immigrant parents, housing, labour matching, etc.. According to previous OECD analysis (OECD, 2014), despite many examples of best practises, Territorial Councils are generally understaffed, have no independent resources, and cannot establish objectives to promote integration unless they attract funding from other sources.

National Co-ordination Work Group: established in 2015 within the Department for Civil Liberties and Immigration of the Ministry of Interior is an example of a multilevel co-ordination mechanism focused on refugee reception and integration mechanisms. The mandate of this work group is oriented towards bridging the reception with the integration phase of recognised refugees and protection status holders and for this purpose it formulated *the National Refugee Integration Plan* (see page 41) released in September 2017. The Work Group is composed of representatives of the Department for Civil Liberties and Immigration, the Department for Public Security both from the Ministry of Interior, the Ministry of Labour, ANCI, UPI and of the Conference of Regions and Autonomous Provinces, as well as the representatives of the Minister for Equal Opportunities, the UNHCR, the National Committee for the Right to Asylum and, depending on the issues on the agenda, the representatives of other administrations and other stakeholders.

This Work Group is considered (Legislative Decree No. 142/2015) a governance tool, for reception and integration of Persons Seeking International Protection. It fulfils different tasks: strategies and plans for reception and integration are approved, sharing and comparing the programming of European Funds, and in particular AMIF, preparing strategies for labour market integration. The Group meets at least three times a year. The guidelines and plans prepared by the National Co-ordination Work Group are implemented locally through Regional Co-ordination Work Groups established within the Prefectures of the regional capitals, which are responsible for planning reception at regional level. This mechanism is conceived to ensure efficient co-operation between the institutions and the bodies in charge of facilitating integration and, in accordance with their remit, monitoring the implementation of the Integration Plan. The regional work group follows the same composition of the national work group (Ministry of Interior, 2017).

Integrated programming between the Minister of Labour and Social Policy (MLPS) – Regions

Since 2014 the MLPS (Minister of Labour and Social Policy) signed 17 Programme Agreements (Accordi di Programma) with the Departments of Labour of the Italian regions. This agreement has the purpose of programming integration activities across levels of government, improve co-ordination across public services, avoid silos and to coordinate the use of financial instruments earmarked for integration purposes, in particular of the EU funding (AMIF, ESF) as described in section 2.1.3 and of the national Migration Policies Fund –Fondo Politiche Migratorie (FPM). However, there are obstacles in implementing these agreements due to territorial disparities, fragmentation of the actors involved and because the different funds (Fondo Nazionale per le Politiche migratorie, AMIF, ESF) that should finance these actions have different timelines (Information provided by the MLPS during OECD field work).

In December 2014 Lazio signed the Programme Agreement with the Ministry of Labour[7]. In 2015 a Regional Integrated plan for socio-labour migrant inclusion (Piano Integrato degli interventi in materia di inserimento lavorativo e di integrazione sociale della popolazione migrante) has been agreed which identifies specific objectives and actions that Lazio committed to implement and the Minister to finance through the Migration Policies Fund (FPM).

In parallel Lazio implemented a AMIF-funded (3 million EUR) project 'Integrare Politiche, servizi ed iniziative per Coinvolgere gli attori e i destinatari (IPOCaD)' *Progetto Multi-Azione FAMI* (. Through this regional programme a governance mechanism has been set up bringing around the same table different regional directorates (social affairs, training and labour) and some pilot municipal districts. The overall objective of the programme is to requalify territorial services to better respond to the needs of migrant, refugee and other vulnerable groups.

Adopting a road-map approach, the project intends to strengthen the capacities of public services to simultaneously respond to multidimensional migrant needs. This implies better co-ordination mechanisms across level and across sectors (health, social, labour). Concretely the project set up territorial *Cabina di Regia* (Steering Committee) – in Rome pilot municipalities are Municipality VII and VIII - involving all the actors including public and private territorial services of inclusion and integration of migrants. These Cabine are in charge of the co-ordination and planning of the actions aiming at improving access to integration services for migrants. The road-map approach culminates in one-stop-shops such as the social-health centres PUA (Punto unico d'accesso) and the job orientation centres (*spazi attivi per il lavoro*, CPIA, COL) where the actions for improving migrants access to services concretise. In Rome the project IPOCAD strengthened two COLs (Job orientation centres) located in the VII and VIII Municipio. Thanks to this project the COLs work as one-stop–shops, where migrants find information about territorial services and are supported by intercultural mediators or agents of territorial development. A monitoring system evaluates the satisfaction of the users (expected beneficiaries for this action are 1 720 migrants), in terms of information received and orientation towards the services that could respond to their needs. The programme, is operational in 15 municipalities across Lazio including Rome and a second phase started in 2019. The sustainability and effectiveness for migrants users of thelinkages between territories and services spurred through this programme has to be assessed over time in order to consider scaling up this experience beyond the pilot municipalities.

Figure 2.1. Institutional Mapping of migrant and refugee integration in Rome

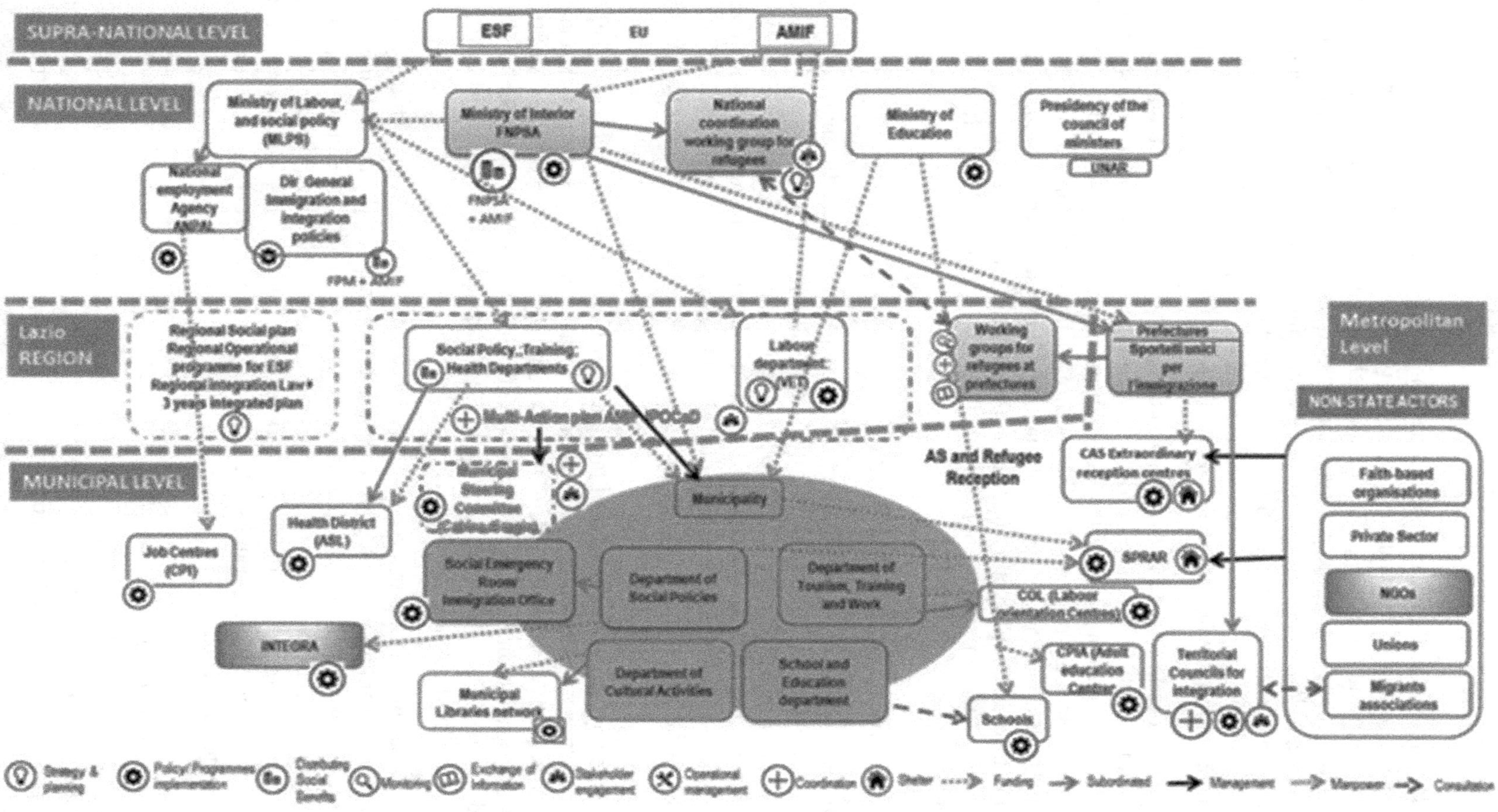

Source: Author elaboration based on information collected from field visit in 2017

Objective 2: Seek policy coherence in addressing the multi-dimensional needs of, and opportunities for, migrants at the local level.

According to 83% of the 72 cities consulted through the OECD Study Working together for local integration of migrants and refugees (OECD, 2018) the policy gap, defined as "sectoral fragmentation of integration-related tasks at central level across ministries, as well as at local level across municipal departments and agencies" is a crucial challenge for migrant integration. Different policy sectors (housing, education, jobs, health, etc.) and related integration-relevant initiatives are sometimes designed using a silo approach, missing cross-sectoral co-ordination and the potential synergies. This section will analyse how the city of Rome seeks policy coherence with regards migrants and refugee integration.

Local authorities in Italy have a very important role for migrants' integration, especially in terms of reception and access to services. Local authorities implement these tasks through their own resources, and through the funds specifically allocated by upper tiers of government. Because of economic balance restrictions and constraints for hiring new personnel, local authorities tend to outsource key services, including for migrant integration, to the third sector, which has historically in Italy a prominent role in the governance system of migrant policy (OECD, 2014) (Chaloff, 2006). Rome follows this pattern.

City vision and approach to integration

Until the early 1990s, while multicultural diversity was increasing, the municipality did not have in place specific measures for migrants. Catholic organisations, associations and Trade Unions provided shelter and assistance to migrants (Alexander, 2017). At the beginning of the 1990s the occupation of the Ex-Panatella factory by more than 2000 migrants of various nationalities attracted the attention of the media and of the public opinion also at the national level, revealing the urgent need for tackling migrants' needs in Rome.

As provided by national and regional law, the City Council ensures access for migrants to general welfare services on the same basis as to all residents. Today, while the City of Rome does not have a specific integration strategy, it provides targeted services related to migrant integration through various departments. Each department has specific objectives related to integration whereas some objectives are cross-department such as Italian language classes (Cavasola, 2014).

Across the sample of cities analysed 54% had developed an overarching strategy to migrant integration. The ambition of integration strategies can vary significantly. While most serve as political programmes, or communication tools, a few also include an action plan, and/or define concrete actions, indicators and responsibilities. Municipalities apply integration strategies as important tools to involve different services (schools, employment agencies, health units, police, etc.) and non-state actors in a more coherent and effective approach towards integration.

Institutional setting for migrant integration coordination at the city level

Decision making is in the hands of the City Council, an elected body, which provides the orientations for all policy sectors to the relevant departments and deliberates on policies. The departments are headed by a director general, non-elected officer. Departments decide whether to implement services directly or to outsource them to external providers through a procurement agreement (see page 52).

Since 1993, the City of Rome established specific units with competence for immigrant policy – today transformed into technical co-ordination groups on migrant-related issues under the responsbaility of the Social Policy, Health and Subsidiarity Department (now called Social Policies Department).

The Technical Co-ordination Offices targeting integration issues are the following:

- The Technical co-ordination office for migrant population deals exclusively with the reception of migrants, refugees and asylum seekers and the assistance to returnees.
- The Technical co-ordination office for labour insertion and professional training for immigrants, refugees and asylum seekers develops actions for this public, in synergy with institutional and NGO services for migrants. This office includes the so-called "Integra" Programme (*Programma Integra*), a social co-operative which has been contracted by the municipality to provide services for migrants and refugees, in terms of legal support, vocational orientation, job counselling, social mediation and housing.
- The Technical Co-ordination office for Roma, Sinti and travellers co-ordinates intervention in favour of these groups.
- The Office for minor protection ensures the adequate reception of unaccompanied minors. The office is in charge of specialised structures for unaccompanied minors and hires social workers for these structures. In the municipal welcoming structure ("Struttura di primissima accoglienza") minors can stay one week and receive a health screening and social workers help them in starting the bureaucratic procedures. After this week, the minors are transferred in a "First Reception Centre" where they can stay 30 days, before being relocated in second level structures. Here the social workers help them in developing their individual project. All these structures are managed by third sector co-operatives.
- Single Desk Service for the reception of migrants at the Immigration Office of the Department has been operational from July 2017 to 2019 - supported by national funding Fondo Nazionale per le Politiche e i Servizi dell'Asilo (FNPSA). This desk integrates services from reception to the following integration steps.

The Department for Social Policies, Subsidiarity and Health, and the Immigration office embedded in it, implement targeted actions in support of migrants, resettled, protection beneficiaries and asylum seekers. These targeted actions do not establish parallel delivery system but rather accompany migrants towards universal services. In particular the work towards the last two categories increased since 2015. The 2015 national law (Decreto Minniti and 142-2015) explained the competences of the different levels of government with regards reception circuits and subsequent changes in the reception system (see page 32).

In addition, as result of the IPOCAD project (see page 32), the Department Tourism, Training and Work steered innovative horizontal and vertical coordination mechanisms for integration in two pilot districts (Municipi VII and VIII). The Territorial Cabine di Regia (steering committees) bring together all private and public actors working on integration related issues (i.e.work, social, housing, health, etc) in those districts and jointly draft a plan to improve services for migrant users. One of the actions agreed is the opening of migrant desks in three Centres for work orientation (COL) operating in these municipalites (see page 54).

From OECD interviews (24 March 2017) with department's officials as well as NGOs operating in this sector, emerged a concern with regard formulating integration actions across silos. The existence of technical co-ordination offices that are 'issue-specific' and respond to parallel funding channels, might hamper a broader approach to inclusion in the city.

In this sense institutional and policy mechanisms could help mainstreaming integration across all policy sectors and avoid parallel migrant-specific structures. Tools could include: i) designing a systematic political response that will mainstream integration into the formulation of all sectoral policies. Vienna is the most exhaustive example of a systematic integration system implemented through contracts that regularly monitor each sector's contribution; ii) establish a service or advisor for migration-relevant issues at the executive level (Mayor office) that will strengthen the coherence among sometimes fragmented pilot experiences and embed a shared vision across all departments. In this sense, the City of Gothenburg and Athens could provide an interesting example.

Utilise consultative mechanisms with migrant communities at local level

In order to enhance policy coherence for migrant inclusion some of the municipalities analysed have developed mechanisms to include migrant communities in the formulation, implementation and evaluation of the policies that concern them.

In Rome as in most other cities analysed, direct political participation of non – EU residents is limited as they do not have the right to vote to municipal elections or to run as local candidates. Currenlty in Rome are no alternative mechanisms to ensure their participation in local decision-making bodies. In 2004, the City Council had established the figure of Adjunct Councillors (Consiglieri aggiunti) to guarantee non-EU migrant participation to local decision makers, which have since then been abolished and currently don't exist. These representatives of migrant communities attended city council meetings and, although they had no right to vote, could raise issues related to migrant integration and anti-discrimination. Also the regional law LR 10/2008 foresees a regional council (*Consulta regionale per l'immigrazione*), which so far has not been implemented in Lazio whereas it exists in other Italian regions.

Migrants also do not frequently organise themselves in formal associations. There are a mere 19 associations (whose composition is made up by 90% of foreign residents) in the Regional Registry of Associations.

Objective 3: Ensure access to, and effective use of, financial resources that are adapted to local responsibilities for migrant integration

In Italy funding for migrant integration at local level depends on national resources, as well as regional and local budgets. EU funding contributes substantially to integration objectives.

At national level, the Law Turco-Napolitano TU 286/1998 established the National Fund for Migratory Policy managed by the Ministry of Labour and Social Policy. Funding was distributed to regions according to criteria such as the number of immigrants and successively distributed to provinces and municipalities according to their programming and projects. In 2001, EUR 56.4 million were spent from this fund (Accorinti, 2013). Since 2003, with the Law L.189/2002, the funds for immigration were absorbed into the National Fund for Social Policy (FNPS)[8] without any earmarking for integration purposes. This fund is directly distributed to regions for ensuring social public service delivery, is not supposed to finance specific projects. Furthermore, the overall availability of national sources for social policy has been progressively reduced (from EUR 825 million in 2006 to EUR 311 million in 2016), implying a reduction of regional and local access to financial resources to provide welfare and social services, including services for immigrants. In general migrants are identified as a target group in most of the social and employment Action Plans formulated by the Ministry of Labour, in particular for those funded through the European Social Fund (see paragraph below).

Overall, national funding for integration has been uncertain and divided across different ministries. In 2007, a new specific fund called "Fund for social inclusion of immigrants" was established, with a total allocation of EUR 50 million. However it was not reallocated in the following years. During the period 2009-2013, the Ministry of Labour and Social Policy allocated EUR 200 million to finance the activities under the five priorities of the "Piano per l'integrazione nella sicurezza. Identità e incontro" "–Fondo Nazionale per le politiche migratorie. In the period 2011-2014 the Ministry of Interior funded services for the integration of migrants (Italian language tests for the Integration Agreement) for a total of EUR 25 million. Furthermore a National Fund for Asylum Policies and Services (Fnpsa) is allocated by the Ministry of the Interior.

With regards to EU funding, the Ministry of Interior is the managing authority for the European Funds for migration, which are becoming more and more substantial.

In the programming period 2007-2013 there were four targeted funds for migration and integration: External Borders Fund (EBF), European Refugee Fund (ERF), European Return Fund (RF), European Fund for the Integration of Third Country Nationals (EIF). The EIF 2007-2013 funded 823 projects for a total expense of EUR 194 million. The main funded sector (40% of the overall expense) was for civic and language training.

In the programming period 2014-2020 the previous three different funds (ERF, EIF, RF) were grouped in a single fund AMIF - Asylum, migration and integration fund. The authority responsible for this Fund is the Department for Civil Liberties and Immigration of the Ministry of Interior, while the Delegated Authority, for the integration component of the fund, is the Ministry of Labour and Social Policies – Directorate General for Immigration and Integration Policy. Italy received EUR 394.18 million for these seven years[9]. Over the same period the EU Commission allocated to Italy EUR 330 million from the Internal Security Fund (ISF) to achieve a high and uniform level of control of the external borders. Up until December 2018, EUR 190 million out of the combined funding for national programmes (EUR 724 million) have been disbursed. On top of this funding, Italy received almost EUR 226 million in Emergency Assistance between beginning 2015 and December 2018, most of which (EUR 170 million) had already been disbursed by December 2018. The AMIF promotes the efficient management of migration flows, improve reception capacities, and a common EU approach to asylum and integration at local and regional level. The AMIF fund represents the main integrated fund for migrants. The integration component of the fund is allocated to regions, municipalities, associations, research bodies to implement projects along four main lines: i) Education (and school dropout); ii) Services for the integration in the labour market; iii) Experience sharing; iv) Strengthening Migrants associations. As mentioned in page 32, the region of Lazio is implementing a programme through AMIF funding (EUR 2 978 000), which takes place also in the municipality of Rome.

The AMIF, as for the previous funds for migrant integration, is complementary to the European Social Fund – ESF. The ESF, within the cohesion policy framework, co-finances regional operational programmes[10] (Piani operativi regionali POR), according to a national unified strategy. Following the objectives promoted at EU level, the ESF can be used to open the European labour market to migrants and ethnic minorities, promoting social inclusion and active social participation of migrants, minorities, refugees and asylum seekers.

Despite these specifics actions, during the phase 2007-2013, migrants were largely underrepresented among the participants in the co-financed programmes.

Only about 5% of the beneficiaries of ESF programmes in the north, 3% in the centre and less than 2% in the south were immigrants, even if in these areas they represent respectively 27%, 20% and 4% of the unemployed (OECD, 2014). The new programming phase (2014-2020) has established an allocation of ESF funds totalling EUR 10 467 million to Italy, with a new, strong focus on social inclusion that must represent 20%, on national basis, of total ESF allocation. As examples, under the Operational programme (OP) 2014/2020 for inclusion two projects were implemented by the Ministry of Labour and Social Policy both funding actions to foster migrants integration in the labour market through internships – one programme (INSIDE)[11] funded 753 internships for refugees in the SPRAR system and a second (PERCORSI)[12] funded more than 2000 internships for unaccompanied minors and young migrants.

Apart from the National Programmes, (e.g.: Social Inclusion, Metropolitan Cities, Education,) regional ESF programmes intervene through Thematic Objectives T.O. (T.O. 8 Employment; T.O. 9 Social Inclusion; T.O. 10 Education and Training). Only TO 9 specifically targets migrants among others vulnerable population, but as any other citizen they can benefit from measures implemented through the others TOs. Particularly, the Regional ESF Programme of Lazio Region (2014-2020) intervenes to support employment, education and training, social inclusion and capacity building, with a budget of EUR 902.5 million of which EUR 180.5 million for social inclusion specifically targeting migrants among other vulnerable populations. There is no specific allocation for local authorities but they can submit proposals by replying to the calls published by the region.

The City of Rome suggested that Managing Authorities could involve cities more directly in the priority setting and implementation phase of EU funds supporting integration measures, in order to break silos across sectoral policies. In particular, the involvement of cities in decision-making regarding the allocation of resources that can be used for integration purposes should make it possible to define integrated strategies for integration at the city level, capable to fully exploit the potentialities of different programmes and funds. In this framework, a specific thematic priority, within Thematic Objective 9 for Social Inclusion, can be a useful solution provided that integration and complementarities with other relevant thematic objectives is actually pursued. A further recommendation to reinforce synergies across EU funds supporting integration is to harmonise the rules attached to different funds. Joint rules and joint programming across EC directorates as well as more specific provisions in EU calls for proposal for cross sectoral proposals would facilitate the possibility to locally develop joint work programmes and incentivise co-ordination of different actions.

Financing at local level to estimate the share of locally-collected resources spent for measures benefitting migrants is a complex exercise. In 2010, ISTAT calculated that, collectively, all Italian municipalities had spent 2.6% (EUR 184 million) of their social expenditure in measures targeting migrants (e.g. residential structures, social workers, intercultural mediators, etc.).

In the city of Rome the expenditures for social services decreased by 6.1%: from EUR 366 million in 2012 to EUR 344 million in 2014. Within this amount the municipality estimates that costs for migrants and Roma users represented 15.8% in 2014, i.e. a 6% increase from

2012. In 2013 the costs for social services related to 'Poverty, adults marginalisation and homeless persons' represented 16.6% of the total social budget, after increasing 5% between 2012 and 2013 this category of costs decreased by 8.4% in 2014. This data show that spending for migrants consistently increased between 2012-2014 while spending for the marginalised and homeless first increased and then decreased over the same period (Metropolitan City of Rome, 2016).

Multi-level governance of the reception and integration mechanisms for asylum seekers and refugees

The legal framework for asylum seekers and refugees

In the last ten years, the national legislation in terms of reception of refugees and asylum seekers has been based on the adoption of European Directives from the Common European Asylum System (CEAS) introduced with the Tampere European Council in 1999[13].

The adapted legislation currently in force in Italy concerns the Legislative Decree 18/2014 (implementing the Qualification Directive) and the Legislative Decree 142/2015 (implementing the Asylum Procedures Directive and the Reception Conditions Directive). A change intervened to the Asylum law (D.L. 286/1998) since November 2018. A new decree (D.L 113/2018) "Security Decree/Decreto sicurezza" makes several changes to the law. In particular art. 1) revoked the possibility to issue termporary permits (two years) based on humanitarian reasons.

Territorial Committees for Asylum examine the asylum requests across the country. Since 2015 with the support of AMIF, the government took measures to expand the capacity of these committees, to guarantee the quality and timeliness of the exam of the international protection applications.

National reception system for asylum seekers and refugees

The evolution of the reception system for asylum seekers and refugees

The reception system for asylum seekers active in post-war Italy consisting of three big CAPS (Assistance Centres for Displaced Persons and Foreigners) resulted insufficient since the late 1980s when Italy went from being a transit country to itself a country of asylum (SPRAR, 2014).

In 1990, CAPS were definitively closed and, with the Martelli Law, refugee assistance was mainly done through the provision of cash support to the refugees for up to 45 days, with little attention to the housing issue.

During the 90s most of the reception was instead supported by civil society and local authorities that created the Italian Consortium of Solidarity in 1992. This co-operation was the basis for what would later become the decentralised reception system for asylum seekers and refugees in Italy.

L. 563/1995 (known as the Puglia law) established three Reception Centres (CDA), renamed in 2006 First Aid Centres and Assistance (CPSA) where identification is done for the expulsion or the recognition of international protection, while L. 40/1998 established Temporary and Assisted Residence Centres (CPTA).

In 1999, the project "Azione Comune" was born, a network of institutional and non-institutional actors supported by the European Union and the Ministry of the Interior, based on the principle of integrated and decentralised reception for asylum seekers and refugees. The aim was to propose a standardised and comprehensive approach of assistance and accompaniment through the provision of services and hospitality in small- and medium-sized centres spread throughout the national territory. In the following years, this approach became the starting point for the Italian reception system, first with the National Asylum Plan (PNA) and then with the Protection System for Asylum and Refugees (SPRAR).

In 2000, following a Memorandum of Understanding signed by ANCI (National Association of Italian Municipalities), UNHCR and the Ministry of the Interior, the PNA was launched. The PNA worked for three years - funded by the European Refugee Fund (ERF) - and it proposed a model of governance and management that underpins the current SPRAR system.

The SPRAR, created with L. 189/2002 (Bossi-Fini), addresses asylum seekers, international protection status holders (Geneva Convention refugees and beneficiaries of subsidiary protection) and beneficiaries of humanitarian protection (until abrogation of this status in November 2018). In continuity with the PNA, the system proposes:

- An integrated reception model, which goes beyond the emergency and assistance logic and is aimed at socio-economic integration;
- Collaboration between different levels of government, from national to local;
- The voluntary participation of the municipalities, which compete to be assigned beneficiaries and corresponding funding from the Minister of Interior;
- The establishment of a territorial network among state and non-state stakeholders.

The Bossi-Fini law also envisaged the creation of Identification Centres (CDI) (later renamed by L. 25/2008 Reception Centres for Asylum Seekers - CARA), for the first phases of assistance and reception of asylum seekers, and the Centres of Temporary Permanence (CPT) (later renamed Identification and Expulsion Centres - CIE and, with the recent DL. 13/2017, Centre for Assisted Repatriation - CPR) to accommodate migrants subject to expulsion orders.

In 2015 Italy introduced the "Roadmap" aimed at implementing the European Agenda on Migration, presented by the European Commission in May 2015 in response to the migration peak. As part of the agenda the CIEs have been converted to Hotspots where EU, UNHCR and Italian authorities operate jointly. In an attempt to alleviate the pressure on Greece and Italy the European Agenda introduced in September 2015 the relocation system: the initial commitment was 160 000 protection seekers are to be relocated in EU Member States within two years (40 000 from Italy and 120 000 from Greece). The total number of people relocated from Italy by end of October 2018 was about 12 700. In total the number of relocated people from Greece and Italy in October 2018 were about 34,700[14].

The current reception system

This paragraph describes the reception system in Italy as governed by Legislative Decree 142/2015 and Italy's 2015 Roadmap (Ministry of the Interior, 2015a), which set the goal of giving an organic structure to the reception system and responding to the demands of the European Union. The paragraph doesn't account for the changes that will follow the implementation of the Security Decree (D.L 113/2018).

The system consists of three phases: identification, first reception, long-term reception

1. **Identification:**

Identification is handled mainly in CIE and, since 2015 converted in hotspots, closed sites where all procedures such as medical screening, pre-identification, registration and photo-identification and fingerprinting are carried out. The hotspots have a capacity of 2 500 places (arrivals in Italy in 2018 were 23,000[15]) and Italians authorities are supported by EU and UNHCR authorities in these operations. On the basis of the results of such activities, asylum seekers will be transferred to first hosting Centres (with the exception of those eligible for relocation to another EU Member State according to the European Agenda on Migration of 2015).

2. **First reception:**

First reception is managed in First reception Centres (i.e CARA, CPSA, CDA and Regionals Hubs) by the Ministry of Interior. These open Centres are involved in the initial reception of asylum seekers assisting them in submitting the application of the "C3 form" (the Asylum application form) to the Territorial Commission. Migrants stay in these Centres for a period of 7 to 30 days before being transferred to the SPRAR/CAS circuit.

3. **Long-term reception:**

The second phase of the reception is ensured by the SPRAR System, and the Extraordinary Reception Centres (Centri di Accoglienza Straordinaria CAS). The SPRAR consists of a network of local authorities, CSOs, third sector entities and associations that set up and run integrated reception projects for refugees, asylum seekers, and humanitarian protection holders. Reception beneficiaries are welcomed into SPRAR structures throughout the length of the examination procedure of the application (theoretically 6 months). In the event of a positive outcome, the beneficiary may remain in the centre for six months, which may be extended for another six.

Because of the peak in asylum seeker arrivals and the congestion of the SPRAR system, since 2014 the CAS system has ensured 77% of total presence in the reception system (Information provided by the Presidency of the Council of Ministers during OECD visit, 2017). The CAS system should provide the same services as the SPRAR Centres, In March 2017, according to the Council of Ministries, 137 855 persons) are hosted in the CAS, 13 385 in CARA/CDA and CPSA, 23 867 are in the SPRAR system while 1 416 are in Hotspots.

The analysis here provided focuses on the long-term reception centres (SPRAR and CAS), which represent steps into which the integration policies can begin. The Italian system, traditionally managed through partnerships across levels of government, since 2015/2016 arrivals evolved towards a more top down approach. The sections below dedicated to sectoral policies, will provide examples of the integration measures offered through the SPRAR and the way they interact with universal territorial systems.

The SPRAR (*Servizio Centrale del Sistema di protezione per i richiedenti asilo e rifugiati*) implementation scheme is structured as follows: the Ministry of the Interior issues a call for proposals asking local entities how many asylum seekers and refugees they are able to host. The previous periodic approach (usually every two/three years) changed in August 2016 and now the call is permanently open to allow more opportunities to establish a SPRAR[16]. The proposals are designed by local authorities and non-state actors and must be in accordance with the directives of the published call and the operative Handbook published by SPRAR Central Service.

Since 2002 the Ministry of Interior has entrusted the management and overall co-ordination of the system to the national association of municipalities (ANCI) (Ministry of the Interior, 2015b). Local administrations issue a public call to identify NGOs (faith based organisations, third sector enterprises, etc.) that are able to deliver the reception in their territory and stipulate framework agreements with the selected ones. Different types of SPRARs are opened according to the different vulnerabilities of their hosts: unaccompanied minors, migrants with mental disabilities, woman alone, etc. SPRAR Centres are funded mainly through the National Fund for Asylum Policies and Services (Fnpsa) allocated by the Ministry of the Interior (Ministry of the Interior, 2015b). Based on data of the Economic and Financial Direction (DEF) of the Council of Ministry, in 2016 expenditures for rescue at sea, health, shelter, and education for asylum seekers and refugees were EUR 3.6 billion (0.2% of Italian GDP), plus EUR 120 million EU funding. This includes costs for reception (SPRAR and CAS systems); in 2016, this represented EUR 2.4 billion. According to the estimates presented by the Ministry of Economy in a scenario with stable arrivals, in 2017 Italy is expected to spend EUR 4.2 billion, or (0.27% of Italian GDP), in total migration costs, of this 68.2% (or EUR 2.8 billion) will be spent for reception. This estimation includes the increase in municipal expenditure directly related to reception (it is estimated to represent an additional 5% of the total SPRAR cost) but does not account for the increase in delivery of services needed for integration and inclusion.[17] In December 2016 the Ministry of Interior issued a National redistribution plan for asylum seekers and refugees (Piano nazionale di ripartizione). According to the plan municipalities should offer a certain number of places in the SPRAR systems according to the following criteria: small municipalities (less than 2 000 inhabitants) host 6 places; the 14 Italian metropolitan areas (including Rome) host 2 beneficiaries for every 1 000 inhabitants; in all other municipalities with more than 2 000 inhabitants, SPRAR places are distributed depending on a regional quota calculated on the basis of the proportion of FNPS (National social funding) that the region receives[18] (Ministry of Interior, 2016). The Ministry of the Interior can ask prefectures to open the extraordinary reception structures (CAS) only in municipalities not complying with this criteria (clausola di salvaguardia)[19].

Regarding CAS, extraordinary reception is implemented through the prefectures. This mechanism does not proceed from interaction with local authorities, often not involved in the identification of the reception structures. In this case, there is no single proposed national call for identifying extraordinary reception centres but rather calls launched by the prefectures in response to specific requests from the Ministry of the Interior[20], in the event that large numbers of migrants do not find places in SPRAR Centres and need to be hosted. There is no criteria established for deciding in which territory the extraordinary facilities will be opened, the decision is taken after consultation of the Prefect with the Department for Civil Liberties and Immigration of the Ministry of Interior, which may order that reception is organised in temporary facilities prepared specifically for this purpose (Ministry of Interior, 2017). CAS, funded entirely by national funds, works similarly to SPRAR Centres except that local authorities are not partners, and management is entrusted to NGOs, private sector and co-operatives. Often these can be the same actors that manage SPRAR facilities. The CAS centres are managed with lower requirements than the ones set in the SPRAR operative manual. Some minimum standards are required in terms of access to language classes, psychological and legal assistance but are often not monitored by prefectures (for more details on CAS standards and monitoring see page 53).[21]

Moving towards a horizon of integration for the persons who have received permits of staying in Italy, the Government released in September 2017 a National Integration Plan for refugees addressing the post-reception phase. This plan aims to co-ordinate existing territorial strategies under a set of national priorities for integrating beneficiaries of international protection. It is a biannual programmatic document, without an action plan or a budget, formulated through consultation with the regional level (for the governance mechanism that formulated the Plan, see page 32). The National Plan defines the implementation guidelines for the actual integration of the beneficiaries of international protection, with special reference to social and work inclusion (also by promoting specific job matching programmes), access to healthcare and welfare, housing, language training and education and anti-discrimination (Ministry of Interior, 2017).

Reception system in the city of Rome

The first municipal reception centres for non-EU citizens in social distress were set up in Rome in the early 1990s, entrusting the management to third-sector social entities through a public call (Fabbri and Saggion, 2014). Initially, the system welcomed a few hundred migrants (mostly Kurds and Yugoslavs), then about 1 800 in 2013 and 3 627 in 2014 (mainly Afghans, Bangladeshis and Sub-Saharan Africans) when the City of Rome joined the SPRAR System.

For twenty years, the reception centres in Rome did not address exclusively asylum seekers and refugees, but non-EU migrants in general. However, in recent years, 80%-90% of the users were international protection seekers and holders.

During the 'North Africa Emergency' of 2011, the national government established the need to distribute migrants throughout the country and the Lazio Region was assigned 5 000 places that were set up in different centres, many of which were in municipalities close to Rome. Although the National Plan exempted the City of Rome because of the high number of migrants already accommodated in the municipality, in 2011 the region through the programme PRIR-Lazio (Regional Project for Social Inclusion of refugees and asylum seekers), in dialogue with local authorities, funded there 14 projects of reception proposed by private operators. In 2013, the city reception system had a capacity to accommodate nearly 2 200 people through the existing system.

The SPRAR in Rome: In 2014, in order to face growing migration pressure, the City of Rome decided to formally join the SPRAR network. In January 2014 the new system was launched, however some of the organisations contracted for its implementation have been under investigation for supposed fund mismanagement. Following these events, the National Anticorruption Authority/ANAC intervened to set up anti-corruption prevention measures and established a permanent co-operation with the City of Rome in order to improve the institutional quality of the administrative procedures. For the 2014-2016 triennium the SPRAR network in the City of Rome had a capacity to host 3 128 people across different typologies of centres: three centres for Unaccompanied Minors; one for people with mental disabilities; 51 ordinary reception centres (Fabbri, 2016; SPRAR 2016a). For the biennium 2017-2019, the Social Policy Department of the city launched a new call (Municipal council deliberation 4072 of 21/12/2016) for two reception projects in SPRAR Centres, an ordinary one for a total capacity of 2 768 people and one for 6 adults with mental disabilities.

In addition, there are 70 CASs in the Metropolitan City of Rome (capacity 3 683; people hosted 4 063 according to the Ministry of Interior data, 19 September 2016).

Figures about the presence of people hosted in the reception centres in Rome change rapidly and it is complex to know the exact number of asylum seekers and refugees in the municipality (Lunaria, 2016). In June 2016 approximately 7 400 asylum seekers and refugees were estimated to be hosted in the Metropolitan City of Rome. Of these 871 people are hosted in the First Reception Centre of Castelnuovo di Porto, 3 603 people in the SPRAR Centres and 2 917 in the CASs (SPRAR, 2016b).

The passage from refugee reception to integration in the City of Rome

In Rome, as is the case in most of the European cities studied, the passage from the reception system, where newcomers are initially hosted and assisted with different services and activities, to finding their place and self-autonomy in their new society, can be very problematic. This discontinuity in Rome is also due to a lack of multi-level co-ordination: the reception and integration policies follow separate funding and management lines. For instance the offer of language courses depends on NGOs both before and after refugee status recognition. However funding for these courses is different as well as their respective standards and there is a lack of co-ordination between them. This translates into a lack of orientation and information for refugees who have to continue their language training.

From the moment of status recognition, refugees, like for other foreigners, have to register as municipal residents which gives them access to the services of the competent territorial district such as economic allowances, vocational education, healthcare or others social interventions. These services are delivered through municipal and decentralised entities (e.g. ASL, CPIA, Schools, CPI, COL). Refugees are unfamiliar with this new system and access to services and opportunities that the city offers is not easy. While in the SPRAR circuit, between 6 and 12 months after recognition, social workers build tailored insertion projects with the refugees, also collaborating with social workers from different municipal departments, this is not always the case for those living in CAS.

The supply of social services and welfare in Italy has been decresing as a consequence of budgetary constraints.These circumstances lead vulnerable groups, including refugees, to turn increasingly to associations or informal networks. Many end up in informal settlements as explained in page 58. For instance, after the reception period in the SPRAR circuit, some refugees can be placed in intermediary structures where social workers accompany them in finding private accommodation. These intermediary structures, or "semi-autonomous homes" run by third sector organisations, only offer a very limited amount of places for recognised refugees. Projects carried out in these institutions focus precisely on trying to accompany refugees towards working autonomously, as well as integrating them into local context through projects involving all citizens as explained in Box 2.2.

> **Box 2.2. Examples of semi-autonomous houses for refugees in Rome**
>
> **"Comunità di Ospitalità Centro Astalli":** since 2015, the faith-based organisation Centro Astalli has launched an innovative semi-autonomy project for refugees to support them in the delicate moment of transition between the reception and the full autonomy. Refugees need to have revenue to reside in the "Cominitá di Ospitalitá", to pay a small rent and provide for themselves. In parallelCentro Astalli developed capacity-building project with 14 religious institutes in the city to spread the "semi-autonomous homes" model. In 2015, the 14 Congregations opened the Hospitality Communities ("Comunità di Ospitalità"), supporting refugees when transitioning from reception systems to self-reliance and working autonomy. In the first year 68 people (55 adults and 13 children) were welcomed in the communities, some of whom, after a few months, can live and work on their own.
>
> Casa Scalabrini 634 (see page 50) is part of the "Welcoming and Inclusive Community" programme of the Scalabrinian Development Co-operation Agency (ASCS Onlus). The house welcomes families and young refugees in semi-autonomy to accompany them on the path of integration. Since June 2015, 85 beneficiaries have been welcomed, 50 of whom have completed the road to autonomy and about 90% of whom have a rental and working contract today. The project, funded by private companies, is not included in any official refugee hosting network.
>
> **Caritas:** in addition to the other refugee and asylum seekers reception projects, Caritas has created two semi-autonomous houses (one for men and one for women). Even in this case, the project aims to support and accompany the search for autonomous employment and housing solutions.

Block 2. Time and space: Keys for migrants and host communities to live together

This section describes the leading principles of the city's reception and integration policies. Across the ten cities analysed in the case studies, the concepts of time and space appear to be essential in conceptualising sustainable solutions. Time is understood as the continuum in which solutions are executed in the city: from day one in the context of short-term reception and orientation, to long-term settling in the city along the key milestones of a migrant and his/her family lives. Space is understood as proximity among hosting communities and newcomers in the city and is well-illustrated by the word "connecting". Different communities can connect around spaces, activities, causes or housing solutions that limit segregation, facilitate regular interaction and break down prejudices and cultural barriers.

Objective 4: Design integration policies that take time into account throughout migrants' lifetimes and evolution of residency status

Use integrated approaches from "Moment Zero/Day One" and entry points throughout migrant lives

It is becoming more and more evident that acquiring a host country language and social norms as early as possible is essential to increase a migrant or refugee's chances to find employment (Bakker, Davegos and Engbersen, 2013; OECD, 2017). The holistic approach that is implemented through the SPRAR system aims at providing newcomers with the right skills as early as possible to facilitate their integration. However, these skills are essential not only to newcomers refugees, but also to other groups with a migrant background who might have been in the city for longer but failed to acquire them. In fact, access to almost every public service as well as participation depends on newcomers' language and cultural awareness. The city and civil society organisations deploy many means and efforts to strengthen migrant language skills as described in page 62.

Access over time can be better achieved by involving actors such as migrants associations, local organisations, labour unions who have longstanding experience in receiving newcomers. Box 2.3 provides examples of existing organisations and associations that provide targeted support to migrants. This partial snapshot already gives an idea of how diffuse the presence of non-state actors is in creating entry points to respond to different needs that migrant might face at various stages of their lives.

> **Box 2.3. Examples of associations providing support to migrants in Rome**
>
> Faith-based organisations have always had a preeminent role, amongst NGOs working for migrants in Rome. The main organisations are: Caritas, Comunità di Sant'Egidio, Centro Astalli, Federazione delle chiese evangeliche in Italia (FCEI), Associazioni cristiane lavoratori italiani (Acli), Associazione Tuscolana Solidarietà (ATS), etc. Services provided span from counselling and information (e.g. "Foreigners Counselling Centre" managed by Caritas), to Italian language and training courses (ACLI offers courses in Italian, English, nursing, computers), from vocational training and entrepreneurship support (ATS' microcredit project for migrant women), to reception and shelter (Centro Astalli manages various reception centres and cafeterias).
>
> Secular organisations are active in Rome in various fields such as: Croce Rossa Italiana (humanitarian activities, legal and administrative counselling, reception Centres), ARCI (providing helpdesks, Italian language courses), Onlus, CIDIS and Asinitas (helpdesks, language classes, vocational training) and independent self-organised associations linked to social urban movements like FOCUS-Casa dei Diritti Sociali, or ESC Infomigrante.
>
> Trade Unions, like FLAI, ANOLF, UIL and CGIL also play a key role. In particular CGIL focuses on economic migrants and it is directly involved in a dialogue with the main Italian institutions (the Ministry of Interior, Prefectures, Police Headquarters) to ensure the defence of migrant rights and advocate pro-migrant legislation. In addition, CGIL has local help desks (Patronati INCA) that provide legal and administrative assistance and information for migrants, helping them in all the paperwork for obtaining a residence permit, asylum or the right to work.
>
> Some migrant associations (e.g. Associna, etc.) also cater to specific nationalities and then refer users to relevant public services facilitating access to universal services. In this regards the Ministry of Labour tried to establish direct dialogue with the young native-born from migrant parents (second generation). In 2014, through a public call, the Ministry involved 30 associations of young second generation migrants in drafting a Manifesto taking stock of their situation and formulating concrete proposals to improve integration or simply to inform public opinion and show their presence and their contribution to society.

Public services also activated a number of entry points for migrants to access services over time as described in page 36. A tighter collaboration could be envisaged between the actors just mentioned in Box 2.3 and the municipal entry points described below. This also would increase the sustainability of the municipal services that are often depending on punctual project financing whereas the faith-based associations and unions have a longstanding presence. An example of municipal and non-state actor collaboration in ensuring entry points for migrants all along their lives is the SAIER service run by the Municipality of Barcelona. In addition a more structured dialogue with migrant associations and NGOs would allow the municipality to grasp the needs of those who operate in the first line for migrants' inclusion and to better targeting its support. In this sense Barcelona offers a good example of structured dialogue with CSOs, receiving their views and coordinating actions sector by sector (i.e dialogue with NGOs engaged in the provision of language classes, etc.).

Provincial Centres for Adults Education (CPIA), see page 63 are an example of entry point activated by the Province of Rome (today Metropolitan City) where migrants, over time, find support for learning Italian as well as vocational training, literacy classes, adult primary and secondary education.

Since 2017 the city is experimenting new entry points to facilitate migrants' access to local public services. In particular the three COLs opened through the project IPOCaD at district level (see page 32) and the One-Stop-Shop for migrant reception opened in July 2017 at the Immigration Office in the municipality of Rome see page 36. The latter integrates municipal services from reception throughout the next steps of the integration path by offering listening, guidance, specialist counselling and planning services, which are all necessary support in the social insertion and active inclusion of migrants. It is meant to orient users to organisations and structures in their territory that can respond to their needs. The project is implemented by the Social Cooperative Europe Consulting in partnership with Programma Integra. The Service was requested by Roma Capitale and financed by Fondo Nazionale per le Politiche e i Servizi dell'Asilo (FNPSA) and will be active until December 2019.[22]

Objectives 5: Create spaces where interaction brings migrant and native-born communities closer

Encourage bottom-up initiatives for creating spaces that foster integration

Proximity to and involvement of the local civil society are key factors for integration. There is a myriad of local, bottom-up initiatives in Rome that help newcomers find their way into the city and that establish spaces that offer meeting points or shelters for migrants, refugees and natives. As mentioned, most of them are the result of associations and faith-based initiatives which sometimes operate also thanks to municipality support.

In particular the SPRAR projects create a link with the territory, to strengthen the local welcoming culture and ease the inclusion of newcomers. For instance, the 'semi-autonomous' houses described in page 47 often organise joint activities between newcomers and existing communities. One example is the Scalabrini House 634[23] in district five of Rome which since 2015 hosted 32 recognised refugees. The House tries to bridge the gaps between newcomers and inhabitants of the neighbourhood, which despite having received migrants for many years, expressed protests against housing centres for refugees. The Scalabrini House organises courses that are open to all inhabitants of the district in tailoring, web-radio speakers, urban agriculture, etc. Open days allow visits in the centre and the guests can engage in actions for active citizenship for instance giving a talk on their experiences in schools and parishes. The project does not receive public funding and is supported by the Scalabrini foundation. Through such activities, asylum seekers and host communities get to know each other from day one, calming the uneasiness that might arise when sudden large numbers of migrants are established in a specific neighbourhood.

Libraries in Rome, like in other cities of the sample, such as in Barcelona, offer places where an exchange between local and migrants is generated. In Rome the exchange happens around language skills (Servizio Intercultura Biblioteche di Roma - Intercultural service in libraries)[24]. With the support of the Department of Cultural Activity of the City of Rome, a network of libraries organises free Italian language classes for migrants that are taught by volunteer teachers. Migrants in turn give Arabic and Chinese language classes to

Italians. Inhabitants of the neighbourhoods participate in these courses for which demand is higher than supply. In fact, there is a waiting list to enrol in classes from year to year. Furthermore, public libraries offer a wide set of intercultural services. A rich catalogue of multilingual books and publications are available in local libraries, each one specialised in local migrant culture, with the aim of preserving bilingualism.

An online portal (www.romamultietnica.it) collects information on multicultural events, news on migrant communities and worldwide literature bibliographies.

To facilitate connections between the host and migrant communities the municipality could engage more systematically with bottom up initiative. One way would be to collect more systematically the information about existing initiatives and identify which type of support the municipality could provide (i.e. availability of public building, communication activities, funding, etc). Amsterdam and Athens offer interesting examples of bottom up initiatives to include migrants that received municipal support.

Block 3. Local capacity for policy formulation and implementation

Objective 6 Build capacity and diversity in civil service, with a view to ensure access to mainstream services for migrants and newcomers

Improve multi-cultural awareness and language skills of the staff of all municipal institutions and companies at all levels as well as increasing diverse ethnic composition serves two objectives: to reflect the characteristics of the city's population and to improve services' accessibility for migrants.

The case study did not collect evidence of a well-established system to develop the capacities of the municipal staff to in order to improve migrants' access to local resources and services. However, there are some significant examples and strategies to move in that direction. For instance one of the axes of the regional Integrated Action Plan for social and labour integration of migrants (see page 29) and the follow up IPOCAD programme aim at strengthening capacities of public municipal service, as well as health and third sector practitioners, in terms of: intercultrual mediation skills, awareness about migrants' rights, obligations and opportunities . The effort to adapt the offer of services to the characteristics of migrants is also reflected in Roman libraries which develop services aimed at a diverse public (see page 50). This has led to an 8% increase in the share of foreigners enrolled in local libraries in 2012. Good example of city's efforts to improve municipal intercultural capacities and diversity can be recognised in the practices established by the city of Berlin and Vienna.

The sector for which capacity-building efforts seem more established is public education where skilled personnel in mediation and language is made available in schools. On the contrary, the case study did not find significant evidence of systematic measures to reduce language barriers and intercultural barriers that migrants might encounter dealing with public administration.for instance at the Single immigration desks, or the municipal services to register local residents. The Immigration office is a step in the direction of ensuring more accessible services for migrants. Examples of a one-stop-shop for migrants where over 10 languages are spoken and documents are translated in several languages can be found in different cities analysed through this study such as Barcelona, Berlin, Vienna, etc.

Objective 7: Strengthen co-operation with non-state stakeholders, including through transparent and effective contracts

Set up co-ordination mechanisms with NGOs, migrants organisations and business operating in the sector

As already described (see page 48) local civil society organisations and faith-based organisations are the protagonists of migrant inclusion in the city (Alexander, 2017). The strategy of the City Council has always been to co-ordinate and outsource to these actors the management of projects and provision of some municipal services, or part of the provincial Piani di Zona for health and social services. These stakeholders also design and implement other projects through regional, national or EU funds and many through private support from charities and foundations. Furthermore, many associations provide several services through voluntary work. The Lazio Region has a registry in which in 2014 were listed 105 associations working on issues related to migrants, 66% of which were located in Rome. These are the official ones, but in fact, many more associations are not institutionalised (Fioretti et al. 2014).

However a permanent body that would structure dialogue and co-ordination between municipal and non-state actors around migrant-related issues does not exist. Although this is foreseen in the regional law, a Regional board for immigration (see page 38) still does not exist in Lazio. Some examples of structured dialogue between the municipality and non-state actors can be found in other cities of the sample such as Barcelona, Paris, etc. In Rome, sectoral co-ordination initiatives have been created by non-state actors. For instance, since 2009 Scuolemigranti Network[25] brings together most of the associations and bodies (100 in 2015) which provide Italian language classes to migrants in the municipality of Rome. This network represents a key and strong actor that has established a direct dialogue with the municipality. This interaction with a network of NGOs allows the municipality to better understand the needs of migrant communities, to disburse funds more effectively and to grant permits to use public schools. Originally established only in the capital, the network has started to expand to other territories in the Lazio region as more migrants move to municipalities outside Rome boosting the demand for language classes.

Set clear contracts and standards in the delivery of services to migrants

The public administration should use clear contracts that allow for learning from past delivery experience, including in emergency situations and which can be adapted when needed. Monitoring can improve the preparedness of local actors and mobilise municipal services to take over outsourced services in case of emergency.

In this sense the City of Rome has strengthened the procedures to outsource contracts within the framework of the SPRAR system, in line with the guidelines of the Anti-corruption authority. Similarly, in March 2017 the Ministry of the Interior adopted the tender specifications scheme for the procurement of the goods and services necessary to the functioning of CAS (Centres for extraordinary reception) that have to be applied by Prefects when issuing a call for bids. for: first aid and assistance centres, first reception centres, temporary facilities and immigration removal centres, with the objective to ensure uniform levels of reception everywhere in Italy. Key points in these specifications include: traceability of the services provided, envisaging a social clause aimed at promoting the stability of employment for the employees.

In order to monitoring of the quality of services' standards the Ministry of the Interior has launched 2 130 inspections in refugees and asylum seekers reception centres, including in extraordinary centres. These activities will supplement the ordinary controls carried out by the inspection teams of the Prefecture. (Ministry of Interior, 2017).

For instance, the City of Stockholm has introduced an interesting example of social clauses that a municipality can embed in its procurement contracts. In their contracts for providing services and goods to the city, private business commit to offer employment and internship opportunities to newly arrived who completed vocational training provided by the Municipal Labour Department.

Objective 8: Intensify the assessment of integration results for migrants and host communities and their use of evidence-based policies

Evaluation at the national level

Under the Ministry of Labour, the Direction for immigration and integration policies produces an annual report on the integration of the 16 most present migrant communities in Italy (Albanian, Bangladeshi, Chinese, Ecuadorian, Egyptian, Filipino, Indian, Moroccan, Moldavian, Nigerian, Pakistani, Peruvian, Senegalese, Sri Lankan, Tunisian and Ukrainian). These reports collect information at the national level about integration in the labour market, access to welfare benefits, participation in unions and financial inclusion[26].

These 16 reports complement the other publications by the Ministry of Labour: the annual National report on migrants integration in the labour market (Rapporto nazionale sui migranti nel Mercato del lavoro), produced since 2010, and the Reports on the presence of migrants in the 14 metropolitan cities of Italy (Rapporti sulla presenza dei migranti nelle 14 città metropolitane italiane), which have been produced since 2016.

In addition the ISTAT (National statistical authority) website allows users to access data on the breakdown of migrant presence by TL3 region (provinces)[27].

These reports and database are a key source for research institutions and universities. The annual report on migrant integration in the labour market is produced together with the ANPAL (Italian Employment Agency) and its release is an opportunity to evaluate migrant-related policy. More generally, the ANPAL conducts an annual survey to assess users' satisfaction with public employment services, such as the customer satisfaction survey for CPI[28] the employment service described page 54. However, further analysis could identify needs for integration indicators across levels of government and ways for making the best use of the information on migrant integration, including across different ministries responsible for areas that affect migrants' lives.

Evaluation at local level

Several research institutes monitor the presence and outcomes of the migrant population in Rome in particular the Osservatorio Romano sulle Migrazioni[29], which has - every year since 2006 - produced a report on the migrant population in Rome that provides key information for local policy makers and others. The report describes the most pressing issues related to integration in the city such as spatial distribution, religion, education, language classes, etc.

The Statistic Operational Unit (Unitá Operativa Statistica) of the City of Rome produces key indicators for both the native and foreign born population such as occupation, unemployment, over-qualification, etc. Also in the annual statistical report of the Metropolitan area of Rome (Metropolitan City of Rome, 2016) many of the indicators are broken down for native and foreign population[30].

From interviews with local NGOs it emerged that data collected from these sources are used as a baseline to formulate project proposals addressing migrant-related issues submitted to local, national authorities or EU funding. There is less evidence regarding the use of this data for policy evaluation and evidence-based policy formulation at municipal level. While data on migrants exist, there is no evidence of a municipal evaluation framework that uses them as a basis to evaluate policies. In addition, such evaluation framework would identify obstacles that this group is experiencing in accessing services or opportunities. It would be important to strengthen the mechanism that makes data on migrant outcomes available to decision-makers who could use such conclusions as the basis for formulating evidence-based policy. This would benefit all inhabitants through inclusive development beyond the very situation of migrant groups. It could be interesting to use evidence-based policy-making mechanisms in Gothenburg and Vienna as examples.

Block 4: Sectoral Measures

Objective 9: Match migrant skills with economic and job opportunities

Migrants' position in the labour market in Italy and Rome

Migration to Italy was initially dominated by labour migration, especially into low-skilled jobs: by 2012, immigrants held one third of these jobs (OECD, 2014). However in 2016 new labour permits declined by 41% compared to 2015 and they represented in that year only 5.7% of new residence permits (ISTAT, 2018).

Rome represents for migrants a major attraction for job placement in the service sector, and for self-employment. According to the 2016 Ministry of Labour report on Metropolitan Rome (Ministry of Labour and Social Policies, 2016) non-EU citizens represented 9.1% of the employed population in this geographic area. In 2013 foreigners' contribution represented 5.4% of total taxes on revenue that the city of Rome collected (addizionale comunale) (Metropolitan City of Rome, 2016). In addition Rome is the city in Italy where more remittances are sent to migrant countries of origin: in 2015 EUR 662.4 million were sent mainly to China, Bangladesh and Philippines even if this represented a 8.4% decrease compared to 2014 (Ministry of Labour and Social Policies, 2016). Although the economic crisis in recent years has dramatically affected Rome and its activities as well, the employment rate in Rome is higher than the Italian average.

It is worth notice that in 2015 in the Metropolitan City of Rome, the employment rate for the population aged between 15-64 was 65.9% for migrant population and 60.7% for native population, while, the same year 12.5% of the migrant population and 10.3% of the native population were unemployed (Elaboration from the Statistical office of City of Rome, based on ISTAT – RFCL). In addition, at national level the native-born employment rate in 2015 was lower than that of foreigners: 56% for native against 58.9% for foreign-born. As pointed out in previous OECD reports (OECD, 2014) "this is a rather unique situation among OECD countries and raises questions about the feasibility of measures targeted towards immigrants in a situation where also the native-born are facing strong difficulties to integrate in the labour market".

Migrants are often hired for low specialised jobs and concentrate in specific fields such as building, transport, catering, commerce, cleaning and caregiving (Centro Studi e Ricerche

IDOS, 2015). In Rome Metropolitan area, the foreign-born population tends to be much more over-qualified for their job than individuals born in Italy. In 2015, 33% of all employed migrants in the Metropolitan city of Rome occupied jobs requiring little or no qualifications despite having a university degree, whereas this number stood at 1.2% of all employed Italians (Statistic Unit, City of Rome). Half of non-EU citizens with a job in the city of Rome are employed in non-qualified manual jobs whereas this figure is 40% at national level and one non-EU worker out of two is paid less than EUR 800 per month. In 2015, 91.3% of non-EU employed migrants worked in the service sector (Ministry of Labour and Social Policies, 2016); 42.4% of total employed migrants in the city worked as caregivers as opposed to 8% of employed nationals in the city (Unitá Statistica City of Rome). In Rome the main pulling economic sectors were the building and commercial, which were hit particularly hard by the crisis and rising unemployment (Centro Studi e Ricerche IDOS, 2016b).

Another popular choice among migrants in Rome is self-employment. However, compared with the past, this choice is more difficult because of the limits in accessing bank loans and the broader recession (Centro Studi e Ricerche IDOS, 2016b). In Rome Metropolitan area migrants represent 18.7% of total individual entrepreneurs registered, this percentage is higher than the national average where migrants represent 10.9% of total entrepreneurs. Mostly migrants set up business in the trade sector (Ministry of Labour and Social Policies, 2016).

Responsabilities across levels of government

Labour market integration policies are a responsibility of subnational governments: the Regione Lazio, the Metropolitan City of Rome and the Municipality. The Metropolitan City of Rome is the institutional level in charge of transposing job policies defined at the central level by the Ministry of Labour, meaning that the Metropolitan authority mostly applies national standards and regulations. Work policies activated in Rome do not have a specific focus on migrant issues (except for the thematic Centres for Orientation to the Labour Market COL described below). For accessing these services migrants need to have a regular permit to stay in Italy.

Labour orientation services in Rome

The city of Rome hosts 5 job centres (Centres for Employment CPI, Centri Per l'Impiego) managed by the region, they refer to a central agency for active labour policy (ANPAL)[31] of the Ministry of Labour. They aim at matching labour demand and supply. The centres assess the competences of the job-seekers[32], and define the path for integration in terms of vocational training and job placement opportunities. These job centres have important administrative responsibilities as they release the certificate of "immediate availability" (DID) for unemployed persons. Non-EU residents with a regular permit have access to CPI's services although there is no specific project targeting them. In the past, the *Centri Servizi per l'Immigrazione* managed by the Rome Province provided for a service of cultural mediation working in synergy with the Job Centres, ensuring a specific attention to migrants. Currently the AMIF Multi-Azione project (described on section 2.1.1) aims at strengthening the CPI's vocation to help integration and they have been involved in the Cabine di Regia.

According to the Job Centre (CPI) database managed by Metropolitan City of Rome, in 2012, 122 401 migrants were enrolled in the CPI lists, representing 8.7% of the total number of the people enrolled. In 2012, 1 364 226 job contracts were finalised through CPI, and 15.6% of them were linked to foreign workers, most of them were non-EU citizens. Migrants were hired essentially for caregiving jobs (46 000 job contracts): most of them were women. While effective for specific job profiles (e.g. caregivers, etc.), it emerged from the interviews with the OECD that the CPI matching mechanisms could be strengthened through a more active involvement of employers who currently do not rely on the CPI to identify their employees, both migrants as well as nationals.

In addition to CPI, since 1997 the Department Tourism-Training-Work of the City of Rome operates and finances 15 Job-Orientation Centres (COL, Centri di Orientamento al Lavoro)[33] offering a wide set of actions for job-seekers such as assistance in consulting job offers, writing a resume, support in business start-up, seminars and training. As opposed to CPIs, the COL does not have the mandate to match the labour offer with the demand. A new information service orients job-seekers for self-employment and microcredit opportunities. In addition to the 15 COLs, there are three thematic COLs, one of which is addressed to asylum seekers and refugees. National and EU funding (FER European Fund for Refugees) finances this specialised centre, which operates within a network of public actors and associations to guarantee an integrated support to refugees. Between 2014 and 2016, this centre facilitated 237 internships for refugees in the metropolitan area and the vast majority (58%) where in the food and beverage sector (Information provided by the Department Tourism-Training-Work of the City of Rome during the OECD visit). Thanks to the IPOCAD project (page 32) three COLs located in the VII and VIII Municipio of the Municipality of Rome opened dedicated Migrant Desks where intercultural mediators attend migrant users. They act as a one-stop-shop orienting migrants on different integration issues across the services available in the territory.

Measures for refugees' integration in the labour market

While asylum seekers have the right to work after 60 days from filing their applications, international protection holders have access to the job market just like Italian citizens.

The SPRAR reception centres have the responsibility to inform the beneficiaries about labour market opportunities, to support them in vocational training and to establish formal agreements with local education and employment services. An example of a pilot action, for refugees in the SPRAR system in Rome, is the action implemented between February and August 2016 by the *Programma Integra*[34] through national funding (INSIDE[35]). To support refugees on the path to labour market inclusion, the programme develops a Personalised Intervention Plan (PIP) based on skills and needs. Some 14 work placements were created and beneficiaries received EUR 500 per month. At the end of the project, 9 of the 14 beneficiaries were offered a job contract (six fixed-term contracts, two on call and one apprenticeship contract). The stipend represented an incentive for employers to initially hire the refugees and then deciding to convert some of them into employee status.

In addition some SPRAR Centres collaborate with the Municipal Job Orientation Centres (COL) in order to activate internships and vocational training courses for refugees. For instance the San Saba Reception Center[36], managed by *Centro Astalli*, with COL Tiburtino and the Faro Foundation, set up training courses and internships that led 15 of the 28 guests of the centre to find a job. The orientation offered in the COL aims at improving refugees' knowledge of the labour market, to raise their awareness about the risk of the informal labour market, and their capacity to choose their professional path, helping them to build a career path by promoting their skills.

Ordinaria Integrazione and Rinnovare l'invito[37] are two multi-dimensional integration projects, each one supporting 70 protection status holders. The projects were funded by the

EU[38] and implemented through a consortium including the Municipality of Rome as well as non-governmental organisations (Integra and Italian Council for Refugees). With regards to the labour market integration component, the project organises internships, skills assessment, professional training courses (i.e. bakery, etc), provides information and guidance. The Direction training-job of the municipality: was in charge of an experimental training aiming at validating previous experience as electricians or mechanics (Percorso sperimentale di validazione delle competenze pregresse). These courses were organised by the city's vocational centres for electricians and car mechanics, to validate the skills of those protection status-holders who had previous experience[39].

National incentives for including refugees in the labour market have been introduced by the budget law 2017[40]. Incentives apply to social co-operatives to employ status-holders of international protection with a permanent contract. The incentive is a contribution, within the limit of expenditure of EUR 500 a year and for a maximum period of 36 months, aimed at the reduction or relief of the compulsory insurance rates due for employees' national insurance and welfare.

Objective 10: Secure access to adequate housing

Housing is a fundamental right for all and for migrants in Rome it represents also a criterion for entering the municipal registration system of the municipality of Rome. Registration in this system is compulsory to have access to the national health system as well as other social services and rights such as family reunification. Not having regular housing can be a barrier to the municipal residence registration. In addition, according to a report by Doctors without borders (Doctors Without Borders, 2016) the municipal registration, or another proof of housing (property contract, loan or declaration of hospitality) are often requested by the police stations in order to issue or renew permits of stay.

Access to housing in the private market

Migrants' ability to access adequate housing is limited, similarly to the situation of migrants in most of the other cities analysed in this study. New dataset compiled by the OECD (Diaz Ramirez, Liebig, Thoreau and Veneri, 2018)[41] and based on previous work by the OECD and the European Union on indicators of immigrant integration (OECD and European Union, 2015) show the gap between migrant and native-born populations in the share of households living in overcrowded housing is greater in urban than non-urban areas (OECD, 2018).

In the private housing market in Rome migrants face higher barriers than natives (CNEL, 2013; AMAR, 2014). They often pay higher rents compared to Italian citizens regardless of their socio-economic status and are asked to give more guarantees, meeting obstacles in obtaining a regular contract, which means they cannot enter the municipal registration system. According to these studies (CNEL, 2013; AMAR, 2014) the main interlocutors - landlords, real estate agents and banks - in the initial phases of house research, are often distrustful of migrants. Often, if migrants cannot succeed in finding a proper housing solution, they can fall into the black market for housing or even resort to squatting.

To respond to this situation, the City of Rome launched a project called AMAR Housing Mediation Agency Rome (Agenzia mediazione abitativa Roma) implemented by Cooperativa Integra[42] to accompany migrants in the search for housing solutions in the private market. This agency supports migrants during flat hunting to overcome discrimination barriers. It provides financial counselling to migrants and cultural mediation training to Italian administrators of residential buildings and migrant tenants to manage cohabitation issues. Created through a project (September 2013 - June 2014) the agency addressed migrants, refugees and asylum seekers. The project established a network at city level with public and private actors supporting the agency's activities. The agency at the end of the project supported 218 migrants, of which 101 for agency activities and 117 for training activities. Two guides were produced for training on intercultural and cohabitation rules and on intercultural communication on social mediation issues.

Access to Public housing

Since the 1980s there has been no increase in public housing stock in Rome. The waiting list for eligible tenants is 17 years. In this context of structural insufficiency it is almost impossible to find a social housing solution for either the native-born population or migrants. There is no legal barrier to access social housing[43] for migrants. The criteria are the same for migrants or nationals: low income, no other home ownership and a residence certificate in the city. Once the flat has been obtained, tenants have to pay a monthly allowance, depending on their income, and their living expenses. The 2008 "Piano Casa" legislation targets migrants with low income who have lived for at least 10 years in Italy and five in the region, as priority beneficiaries of social housing, but this law was never implemented in Rome.

Temporary housing solutions

In the absence of a policy framework to develop long-term solutions, the city has put in place residual actions to find emergency housing. Although not specifically addressing migrants but vulnerable groups in general, many migrants have benefited from these solutions.

i) 33 Temporary Housing Centres (CAAT, Centri di Assistenza Alloggiativa Temporanea) were used since 2005 hosting 2 000 households who had been evicted from squats. Their temporary housing became permanent, and people remained in CAAT for years. Because of the high cost of management and maintenance for the municipality, the City Council decided in 2013 to start closing these centres. Since then eight of Centres have been closed, evicting 160 households. In March 2017 1 700 households remain in CAAT. People who have been evicted from the CAAT are entitled to a "house voucher" (Buono Casa) which varies according to family composition and can partially cover rents.

ii) Residenze fittizie (Fake Residence), which was initially thought as a measure for homeless individuals, also allows undocumented migrants and Roma to have a physical, legally-recognised address in order to proceed to municipal residence registration and have access to services (e.g. access to social and health services, etc.). This municipal programme allows people without a stable residence or living in squats to ask for a temporary residence in "Via Modesta Valenti", a fake address. To obtain the municipal registration the person has to enrol in a social programme run by one of the authorised associations or by the public social services. The district's social services must check the applicant's living condition within 5 days from the request. Once the applicant obtains the residency document registered in "Via Modesta Valenti", he/she must keep in touch with the social services for a year, and demonstrate the permanence of the state of need.

Beyond municipal housing interventions, it is important to mention the common recurrence of squatting of private or public buildings. Historically in Rome a number of organisations have claimed their housing right by squatting unoccupied buildings in the city. At present, it is very frequent for migrants to live in squats. In 2016 a report by Doctors without Borders (Doctors Without Borders, 2016) identified 2 250/2 880 asylum seekers and holders of international and humanitarian protection who have not been included in the institutional reception system and live in squats and informal settlements in the city of Rome. Some of these squats have been subject to evictions (e.g. Ponte Mammolo in May 2015, Baobab Centre in Via Cupa in November 2015).

Access to housing for refugees and asylum seekers

As explained in page 41, while waiting for the decision of the Territorial Commission on their status, asylum seekers are hosted in the reception centres of the National Protection System (SPRAR, CAS or in other reception Centres) in the city of Rome. Once international protection has been obtained, the beneficiary may ask for hospitality in the Centres for another 6-12 months.

At this stage, the entity managing the centre provides beneficiaries with guidance concerning the real estate market, and assistance in finding temporary solutions until they can afford a permanent self-sustained accommodation. Once out of the reception system and despite having a residence permit, most of the refugees, however, struggle to enter the housing market.

Objective 11: Provide social welfare measures that are aligned with migrant inclusion

The Social Policy, Health and Subsidiarity Department of the City of Rome is, see page 36, the department most involved in integration-related activities. The department is in charge of providing the following social services to migrant and non-migrant population:

- Basic Social services: shelters, social cafeterias, clothing, showers, etc. The Department manages the "Sala Operativa Sociale" (SOS) which receives social alerts from people in need of shelter among other urgent needs. During winter it operates a day and night shelter (Piano freddo) for homeless persons whether Italian nationals and foreigners.
- Immigration office dealing with all aspects of migrant inclusion: information and orientation; reception; legal assistance; information on Italian language courses, vocational training or labour insertion. Since July 2017 this service hosts the One-Stop-Shop for migrant reception (see page 36).
- Unaccompanied minors (see page 36)
- Disability, the elderly, people with dependences.
- Social assistance to homeless: besides in-kind assistance (shower, laundry, cafeteria) the Department's social workers define individual projects for homeless people.

This municipal office operates within a network of public - regional authorities (ASL, etc.) - and non-state actors who are engaged in the provision of health and social services to migrants such as Consorzio Roma Solidarietà (Caritas Diocesana di Roma), Association and Foundation Centro Astalli; Comunità di Sant'Egidio, Centro Welcome, CIES Centro Informazione e Educazione allo Sviluppo, Association Focus Casa dei Diritti Sociali, Association Medici contro la Tortura, Association for promoting and defending rights Erythros, ACSE Association Comboniana Servizio Emigranti e Profughi, Association Solidarietà Vincenziana, SRM Servizio Rifugiati e Migranti, FCEI Federation of Evangelic Churches in Italy and Save the Children Italy[44]. They offer social services such as information and orientation desks, counselling centres, reception centres, day centres, cafeterias and health points.

Municipalities are in charge of disbursing the national welfare/poverty allowance (Reddito d'inclusione that was introduced since 2018)[45]. The municipality collects the application that is approved and processed by the National Welfare Institute (INSP). This allowance is disbursed to households, with at least one minor or a person over 55-years who is unemployed, based on revenue. Non-EU and EU residents can access it if they have lived for at least two years in Italy, and non-EU only if they hold a long-term residence permit. International protection beneficiaries can receive this entitlement as well. A number of bureaucratic procedures and certificates (e.g. ISEE 2018, etc.) might complicate migrants' access to this measure, particularly if they cannot benefit from linguistic support. This allowance lasts for 18 months and is accompanied by personalised advice from the municipality or the public employment agency and address the entire household. In early 2019 a new allowance 'Reddito di Cittadinanza' (Citizenship revenue) has been approved by the Italian Parliament and it will replace the Reddito d'inclusione. This allowance will be disbursed by the Job Centres and applies to third-country national with a long-term residence permit who lived at least 10 years in Italy of which the last two years continuously[46].

Health services

Legal access to health is guaranteed by law to all

Since the 1990s, Italy has guaranteed universal access to health services to all citizens. The Dini Law[47] in 1995 and then the TU 286/1998[48] state that migrants living in Italy with a regular residence permit have the right to enrol in the National Health System (Sistema Sanitario Nazionale, SSN). This right is also extended to individuals who are temporarily undocumented.

Local social and health service provision can be characterised as a mosaic of different experiences across Italy as regional and local institutions are in charge of defining and providing social and health policies. In particular, regions govern and manage every activity related to health service delivery.

Since 1997, the Lazio Region set up a legislative framework for migrant health issues[49], transposing the national law on migrant healthcare into regional regulation. In Lazio, migrants with a residence permit should enrol in the SSN. The enrolment needs to be renewed periodically depending on the residence permit typology and gives access to healthcare on the same basis as Italian citizens. Special attention is devoted to migrants in transit (Stranieri Temporaneamente Presenti, STP), who receive urgent or essential care even if they are undocumented. In Lazio, migrants from the EU can access emergency health care that cannot be put off, and they are registered as "not enrolled" (Europeo non iscritto, ENI) (Regione Lazio, n. 26146, March 2008). Lazio provides access to healthcare to asylum seekers and refugees[50] for 12 months renewable until the expiry date of their permit of stay. Requests to enrol in the SSN have to be registered at the health district where migrants are residents. Until the moment they are not registered as resident in a municipal district, neither regular migrants nor asylum seekers/refugees can enrol in the SSN. However, according to a recent report there is a gap between the right to access health services and the real exercise of this right, partially due to the lack of assignment of municipal residence registration for all those living in informal accommodations (Doctors Without Borders, 2016). Beyond the administrative obstacles, migrants lack information about their right to access health services or fear to do so when they are irregular. This results in poor access to prevention and early diagnosis care, undermining the benefits of their constitutional right to healthcare.

Health Services targeting migrants in Rome

Besides establishing the right to universal health services, Lazio Region also sets by law specific measures to facilitate migrant access to health services. For instance, cultural mediators should be present in each regional health service (Regione Lazio – Assessorato alla Sanità Prot. 3151/44/09, January 2004), their activities are: orientation, information, linguistic, social and communicative facilitation.

The ASL (Azienda Sanitaria Locale) Health District in charge of the centre of Rome (Roma 1) managed by the region, operates seven clinics specialised for non-EU citizens or for EU citizen with the ENI code. Also migrants who are not residents in this area can access these clinics. Clinics provide basic healthcare and can prescribe drugs. ASL Roma 1 also operates a specific clinic for women, especially if they do not have a residence permit.

The San Gallicano hospital (Box 2.4) is an example of a dedicated structure for migrants that offers an integrated model of assistance.

Box 2.4. The San Gallicano Hospital and the National Institute for Migrant Health Promotion

The INMP (National Institute for Migrant Health Promotion) represents an example of multi-level co-ordination between the Ministry of Health and regions. Created by law in 2007 the Institute was identified as the national referral centre for social and healthcare issues related to migration and poverty and for transcultural mediation in the healthcare field. The Institute's staff is composed of doctors, nurses, psychologists, anthropologists, and transcultural mediators. The institute assists migrants in different settings: primary assistance in areas where mass arrivals occur under the supervision of the prefectures and thanks to the EU-funded project CARE in partnership with Greece, and Croatia, initial process of social inclusion in metropolitan areas in structures such as the San Gallicano Hospital in Rome. The Institute has experimented and developed an integrated model where medical anthropologists, psychologists with an ethno-psychiatry background, and cultural mediators work together to offer tailored and accessible healthcare services, delivered by the SSN. The clinic also helps migrants in orienting themselves from a bureaucratic point of view, referring them to the proper health assistance they need in Italy as foreigners. The INMP established collaboration protocols with Sicily, Puglia, Lazio and progressively with other Italian regions.

Source: www.inmp.it/index.php/ita/Servizi-Socio-Sanitari; www.inmp.it/index.php/eng/Projects/The-CARE-Project.

In general, psychological care is limited in public health services in the city for these vulnerable categories as well as for Italian citizens. A significant exception is SA.MI.FO. (Salute Migranti Forzati)[51] a specialised structure that offers psychological health care to migrants, refugees, asylum seekers, victims of torture and violence. This interdisciplinary team operates within the structures of the ASL Roma 1 and in association with Centro Astalli. The team orients directly the users to specialised public medical services (e.g. gynaecology, orthopaedic, general practitioners, psychologist, etc.) and connects them with the social services available in the territory. In 2016 the SA.MI.FO. helped 2 000 persons, most of whom were referred by the associations and reception centres of the territory.

The city of Rome also develops health plans to support some vulnerable categories (e.g. the Roma population in the city) through municipal services. These plans could benefit from closer co-ordination with the regional health departments that also take measures towards the same groups.

Objective 12: Establish education responses to address segregation and provide equitable paths to professional growth

Learning Italian for adult migrants

Learning the language of the country chosen as a place to live is a fundamental step for improving the social inclusion of migrants. For those who arrive after schooling age this requires access to adult language classes. Non-EU migrants applying for a residency visa for more than one year are expected to achieve A2 European level according to the Integration agreement introduced in 2008 and operational since 2012 (see page 24). Migrants have access to free language classes at local level. The classes are offered through the adult education centres (CPIA system) created by the Ministry of Education in 1997. Local authorities rapidly integrated the CPIAs into their existing offer for migrant language training and slowly ceased to sponsor language classes provided by the third sector to provide additional funding to support the ministry-paid school teachers (OECD, 2006).

Italian language classes for migrants are offered in Rome by:

Provincial Adults Education Centres (*Centri Provinciali per l'Istruzione degli Adulti*, CPIA) previously CTP Territorial Lifelong Learning Centres (*Centri Territoriali Permanenti*)[52]:

There were 17 different CTP in the municipality of Rome, which were reformed in 2012 and were grouped into four CPIAs. These centres are under the authority of the Ministry for Education, which assigns elementary and middle school teachers to adult education, including for foreign residents. The centres offer basic language skills courses, language integration certificate courses and middle school certificate classes. The latter are important for immigrants as they are usually a prerequisite for enrolment in publicly-funded vocational training courses (OECD, 2006). The CPIAs organise the language tests that non-EU residents take to obtain the long-term permit and the civic orientation class that they have to attend within two months after signing the Integration agreement. Non-EU migrants who attended the language courses at CPIA and obtained an A2 certificate or obtained the middle school certificate do not need to take the test[53]. Between June 2013 and May 2014, CTPs in Rome provided courses to 41.7% of the total foreign residents (27 310 students) enrolled in language courses in the capital (Roman Observatory on Migrations, 2016). Some of the classes offered in CPIA are called Co-ordinated classes (*Corsi co-ordinati*) and are held by associations. During the period 2011-2013 funding was provided by the Lazio region through a European Integration Fund (EIF) grant. During this period, the programme (PRILS LAZIO) provided funding for Italian classes to foreign residents, and training for social workers. It enrolled 1 276 migrants in CTP and 1 020 of them obtained the A1 and A2 degree; 673 students attended the Co-ordinated courses held by the third sector in CTP spaces and 538 of them obtained the A1 and A2 degree. After this funding period, CPIA continue to be partially funded by European funds (AMIF).

Third sector organisations:

Between June 2013 and May 2014, 58.3% of the foreign residents who received language classes in Rome attended classes taught through volunteer network. As mentioned in page

52, organisations providing free language classes to migrants, are represented in the main local network "Scuolemigranti". They provide classes to adults and children as well, hosted in public school or association spaces. In Rome, the third sector provides most of the offer of language classes. However one has to keep in mind that outside the capital, in the rest of Lazio region, volunteer organisations represent only 18.4% of the offer of language courses for migrants whereas public offer represent 81.6% (Roman Observatory on Migrations, 2016).

Currently it is estimated that the public offer in Lazio and in Rome remains insufficient to address the migrants' demand for language classes (Roman Observatory on Migrations, 2016). In the capital, the combination of public and association offers still leaves around 30-60% of the demand unmet (Venanzetti, 2015). When CPIA were introduced the public system seemed to have achieved better co-ordination and competition as compared to the previous third-sector driven supply of language courses, often unco-ordinated and without a clear certification mechanism (OECD, 2006). However, there are not enough language courses offered in Rome. Public service capacity to deliver language classes could be improved by strengthening co-ordination across levels of government. Streamlining national and EU resources available across levels, through a joint programming cycle and indicators between the Ministry of Education, the Region and the municipality could be considered. A more performant public language system would enable migrants to meet their legal obligation to learn Italian much more easily.

In parallel, third sector entities providing language classes in Rome achieved better co-ordination by setting up 'Scuolemigranti' (see page 52). This bottom-up network seems effective in co-ordinating the offer available and establishing direct dialogue with the municipality (e.g. obtaining funding and the permission for using school spaces). Many associations (religious, secular, related to unions, parish, etc.) in this network have formed strong relationships with migrant associations, for instance the Association PerCorsi that is linked to the Sikh community. Scuolemigranti also facilitates the co-ordination of volunteer associations providing language classes in the municipalities outside Rome. A positive result is that the classes become a social moment beyond ethnic groups and allows groups of different nationalities to meet each other (Roman Observatory on Migrations, 2016). In addition associations (e.g. Caritas, etc.) can provide language training also to undocumented migrants who are not officially allowed to enrol in CTPs.

For adult asylum seekers and refugees:

The SPRAR Operational Handbook foresees a minimum of ten hours per week of Italian classes for the persons hosted in the structure. It is the responsibility of the organisation managing the SPRAR to find Italian courses available in the territory (CPIA, schools, and third sector), and to provide transport, or to organise the courses themselves.

Education for children enrolled in public schools

Key indicators

In 2015 non-EU pupils enrolled in the schools of the city of Rome totalled 34 118 or 5.6% of the total number of pupils enrolled in Rome schools. In the 2014/2015 school year, 39 922 foreign students attended public schools in the Metropolitan City of Rome: 34.9% were enrolled in primary school, 26.3% in high school, 20.3% in middle school and 18.4% went to preschool (Centro Studi e Ricerche IDOS, 2016b). They represented 10.1% of total students (10.8% in preschool, 10.9% in primary school, 10.8% in middle school, and 8.5%

in high school) whereas at national level foreign pupils represent 7% of total students in public schools. The Italian peculiarity is that among these numbers, 51.2% were born in Italy but are still considered foreigners and will access the citizenship only at age19 under current legislation. Out of 3 000 schools in Rome (all levels considered) only 19% did not have non-EU pupils among their students according to the Ministry of Labour and Social Policies (2016).

In the City of Rome, there is a different trend compared to the rest of the country in terms of the typology of high schools that foreign students tend to attend. In fact, students of high schools who are foreigners (almost 5% of total high school students in Rome), are divided equally between technical schools (38.6%), 'lyceums' scientific or literary high schools-(36.4%) and professional schools (25%). This is not the case in the rest of the country where foreign students concentrate in technical and vocational schools (2014/2015, data of the Ministry of Education; Centro Studi e Ricerche IDOS, 2016b) (OECD, 2014). This data could suggest that in Rome a more inclusive dynamic towards foreign students is occurring, facilitating their access to university or skilled jobs.

National policies for children with migrant background in public schools

Italy was one of the first countries to develop an intercultural approach in the school system, partly because many Italian migrants who were coming back to Italy were not able to speak proper Italian. Italian schools have a long tradition in welcoming "foreigners". The term "intercultural education" appeared for the first time in the official programmes for the Italian lower secondary schools in 1979. In 1985, the intercultural approach was also applied and implemented for primary school students. In the 1990s, with the primary school reform, inter-culturalism was included in the guidelines for kindergartens and in 1992 it was also included in programmes for the upper secondary schools. To support this process, the Ministry of Education (MPI – MIUR) instituted a special office in 2004, the General Direction for Students (Direzione Generale per lo Studente) with a sector specifically dedicated to the inclusion of foreign, Roma and Sinti children. In 2006, the same Ministry began supporting the creation of the "Osservatorio Nazionale per l'integrazione degli alunni stranieri e per l'educazione interculturale" (National Observatory for the integration of foreign children and for intercultural education), involving experts and representatives of the NGOs.

The national level has the competence for defining school and education policies and their ultimate scope. Schools receive the content of teaching programmes from the national level. However, since the 2001 decentralisation reform some of the national competences were transferred to regional and municipal level. For instance these levels now define the distribution of schools across the territory, the school calendar, the right to education (scholarships, etc.). This adds to their responsibility to offer logistical support and ownership of school buildings[54]. With regards to adult education, since the decentralisation reform, this competence was transferred to provincial and municipal levels.

Currently in each school with foreign pupils, the national educational system provides for qualified teachers of Italian as well as cultural mediators. However, for accomplishing at their best their educational and integration role, schools are looking for additional funds and specifically trained teachers. The ISFOL survey carried out in 2013 noted that there was no national strategy for providing intercultural training courses for teachers (OECD, 2014).

Projects and initiatives fostering migrant pupils' integration are promoted by single schools or third sector bodies (see examples below by Scuolemigranti in Rome). Schools or districts can apply for additional funding to implement actions aiming at integrating migrants. This funding is provided by the Ministry of Education (Law 440/1997), the AMIF, managed by the Ministry of Interior, and the FEAD (Fund for European Aid to the Most Deprived), managed by Ministry of Labour.

Offer of education for pupils with a migrant origin in the City of Rome

All children under 16 years of age must be guaranteed access to schools regardless of their legal status and even without all necessary documents. Asylum seeker and refugee children are included and it is the responsibility of the entities that manage SPRAR and CAS Centres to create a partnership with schools in order to guarantee the right to education and encourage inclusion and school attendance.

In addition to ensuring access to school, the Education Department of the city of Rome also funded additional activities to improve the integration of foreign pupils in public schools. The municipality funded punctual intercultural activities and training for teachers in particular for preschool teachers and day-care staff. Examples of projects providing cultural mediation in public schools funded by the municipality are "Progetto Aquilone" Project Kite, "Accogliere per Integrare" Welcoming for Integrating Project, (school year 2011-12).

A scuola con il mondo – implemented by Programma Integra[55] is a project that is operated in primary schools through theatre workshops run by intercultural mediators. The main objective of this project was to recognise and to celebrate differences, helping students in relating with issues such as immigration, stereotypes and prejudices. Another project on multicultural integration implemented in eight high schools in Rome and funded by the Ministry Interior and the European Fund for Integration (2009) is the Progetto Jambo[56]. The project aimed at promoting organic actions for social, educational, professional integration of young migrants. Schools offered workshops and Italian classes as a chance for socialisation and learning in a positive context.

In addition to the municipal services, non-state actors, grouped in the network Scuolemigranti promote workshops and projects in schools at all levels and receive special funding from the EU or the region. Increasingly at the request of public schools in Rome, associations that are members of this network offer intercultural and linguistic workshops, after-school services and meetings with the families. The linguistic workshop offered by Scuolemigranti in 70 public schools in Rome between 2013 and 2014 included 4-6 hours per week for small groups of students (6-8 pupils) for up to three teachers. For those students who enrol during the school year the workshop was more intensive (10-12 hours per week). Communication with the rest of the students is a priority to explain the situation of their new classmates. Intercultural education for classes at all levels is also provided by associations, involving artists and members of foreign communities. Associations also provide intercultural mediators who can speak the parents' mother tongue and facilitate their interaction with teachers. The network also organises after-school workshops that often become places of reference for neighbourhood life with theatre, games and other activities organised (Roman Observatory on Migrations, 2016).

In general the passage from school to work of immigrant offspring has not received enough attention yet in terms of national policies. Associations of second generation youth are working to raise awareness of better integration of immigrant offspring in the Italian job market (OECD, 2014). Currently the City (Direction Training and Labour) offers vocational training for young students between 14-18 years. While they don't target migrants, many pupils are first and second generation migrants. Through nine Centres for Vocational Training (Centri Formazione Professionale CFP) vocational free training is offered in the sectors of industry, crafts, tourism and services. Courses are aimed at job placement and they are recognized and funded by the Lazio Region.

Public education for adult migrants:

In addition to the literacy and language classes described above, the Provincial Adults Education Centres (CPIA) can offer adult migrants as well as all other publics the following courses:

- courses to complete the primary education level;
- courses to complete the secondary education level;
- courses for students sixteen years of age and older having completed middle school, who are not able to attend daily lessons.

With regards to vocational training, some specific projects addressed migrants in particular such as the ones promoted by a third-sector operator Programma Integra[57].

Notes

[1] www.integrazionemigranti.gov.it/en/legal-framework/domestic-law/Pages/Integration-Plan.aspx.

[2] www.integrazionemigranti.gov.it/en/latest-news/highlights/Pages/Integration-agreement.aspx.

[3] www.integrazionemigranti.gov.it/Attualita/Approfondimenti/Pagine/Le-comunita-migranti-in-Italia--Dati-al-primo-gennaio-2017.aspx.

[4] www.integrazionemigranti.gov.it/Areetematiche/PaesiComunitari-e-associazioniMigranti/Pagine/mappatura-associazioni.aspx.

[5] http://www.projectaida.eu/wp-content/themes/thunderbolt/docs/Sintesi-dei-modelli-organizzativi-dei-Distretti-italiani.pdf.

[6] www.cittametropolitanaroma.gov.it/.

[7] http://www.integrazionemigranti.gov.it/leregioni/lazio/Pagine/Piano-integrato-di-intervento-regionale.aspx.

[8] http://www.lavoro.gov.it/strumenti-e-servizi/Fondo-nazionale-politiche-sociali/Pagine/default.aspx.

[9] https://ec.europa.eu/home-affairs/sites/homeaffairs/files/what-we-do/policies/european-agenda-migration/20181219_managing-migration-eu-financial-support-to-italy_en.pdf.

[10] The objectives are set out in the ESF Plans of Action for Lazio and include specific priorities in allocating resources (except for Axis 5, not priority), and in particular: Axis 1 - Employment (EUR 414 153 326); Axis 2 - Social Inclusion (EUR 180 500 000); Axis 3 - Education and training (EUR 238 500 000); Axis 4 - Institutional and administrative capacity (EUR 33 280 000); Axis 5 - Technical assistance (EUR 36 101 388).

[11] http://www.integrazionemigranti.gov.it/Progetti-e-azioni/Pagine/INSIDE---INSerimento-Integrazione-NordSud-inclusionE.aspx+.

[12] http://www.integrazionemigranti.gov.it/Progetti-e-azioni/Pagine/Percorsi-di-integrazione-socio-lavorativa-per-minori-non-accompagnati-e-giovani-migranti-.aspx.

[13] In 2007, the second phase of the implementation of the CEAS was launched: Strategic Asylum Plan (2008) aimed at harmonising the standards of protection and co-operation between Member States; Regulation 2013/604 / EU (Dublin III); the Asylum Procedures Directive (2013/32 / EU) aimed at speeding up the procedures for international protection recognition; Reception Conditions

Directive (2013/33 / EU) aimed at harmonising the reception conditions in the different Member States; the Qualification Directive (2011/95 / EU).

[14] https://ec.europa.eu/home-affairs/sites/homeaffairs/files/what-we-do/policies/european-agenda-migration/press-material/docs/state_of_play_-_relocation_en.pdf.

[15] https://data2.unhcr.org/en/documents/download/67726.

[16] www.sprar.it/wp-content/uploads/2017/02/ministrointerno11ottobre2016.pdf.

[17] http://www.rapportiparlamento.gov.it/question-time/26-luglio-2017-camera/padoan-nel-2017-prevista-una-spesa-di-4-2-miliardi-per-soccorso-e-accoglienza-dei-migranti/.

[18] www.regione.fvg.it/rafvg/export/sites/default/RAFVG/cultura-sport/immigrazione/news/Piano_Ministero_Interno_17_genn_2017.pdf.

[19] www.sprar.it/piano-di-ripartizione-e-clausola-di-salvaguardia.

[20] Based on an agreement on 10 July 2014: the number of migrants in the regions is equal to the share of the National Fund for Social Policies (FNPS).

[21] www.sprar.it/guide-normative/decreti-e-circolari.

[22] www.integrazionemigranti.gov.it/Newsletter/Documents/newsletter/inglese/INGLESE.pdf.

[23] http://scalabrini634.it/.

[24] www.romamultietnica.it/italiano-per-stranieri-in-biblioteca.html.

[25] www.scuolemigranti.org/.

[26] www.integrazionemigranti.gov.it/Attualita/Approfondimenti/Pagine/Le-comunita-migranti-in-Italia--Dati-al-primo-gennaio-2017.aspx.

[27] www.istat.it/it/lazio.

[28] http://www.anpal.gov.it/Dati-e-pubblicazioni/Pagine/Indagine-sulla-customer-satisfaction-dei-Cpi-2018.aspx.

[29] www.dossierimmigrazione.it/catalogo/Indice%20-%20Osservatorio%20Romano%20sulle%20Migrazioni%20XI%20Rapporto.pdf.

[30] www.cittametropolitanaroma.gov.it/homepage/ufficio-statistica/pubblicazioni/rapporti-annuali-2/.

[31] www.anpal.gov.it/Cittadini/Sistema%20Duale/Pagine/default.aspx.

[32] www.anpal.gov.it/Cittadini/Profilazione/Pagine/default.aspx.

[33] https://www.comune.roma.it/web/it/scheda-servizi.page?contentId=INF39031.

[34] www.programmaintegra.it/wp/programma-integra/progetti/inside-inserimento-integrazione-nordsud-inclusione/.

[35] INSIDE – INSerimento Integrazione NordSud inclusionE, funded by National Migration Policies Fund in 2013, aims at the socio-occupational inclusion of refugees hosted in the SPRAR network.

[36] http://centroastalli.it/servizi/centro-san-saba/.

[37] www.integrazionemigranti.gov.it/EsperienzeSulTerritorio/protezioneinternazionale/Documents/progetto%20Ordinaria%20Integrazione.pdf.

[38] Annual Programme 2013 of The European Fund for Refugees (FER Action 1)

[39] www.integrazionemigranti.gov.it/EsperienzeSulTerritorio/protezioneinternazionale/Documents/progetto%20Rinnovare%20l%27IN%20VI%20TO.pdf.

[40] www.integrazionemigranti.gov.it/Newsletter/Documents/newsletter/inglese/INGLESE.pdf, Article 1, paragraph 109.

[41] Regional integration indicators were produced jointly by the Economic Analysis, Statistics and Multi-Level Governance Section (CFE) and the International Migration Division (ELS).

[42] www.programmaintegra.it/wp/programma-integra/progetti/progetto-amar-agenzia-di-mediazione-abitativa-di-roma/.

[43] Immigration Law from 1998 Testo Unico Immigrazione, art. 43, comma 2, lettera c.

[44] www.aslroma1.it/migranti.

[45] http://www.lavoro.gov.it/temi-e-priorita/poverta-ed-esclusione-sociale/focus-on/Reddito-di-Inclusione-ReI/Pagine/default.aspx.

[46] https://www.redditodicittadinanza.gov.it/.

[47] DECRETO-LEGGE 18 November 1995, n. 489 "Disposizioni urgenti in materia di politica dell'immigrazione e per la regolamentazione dell'ingresso e soggiorno nel territorio nazionale dei cittadini dei Paesi non appartenenti all'Unione europea"

[48] Decreto Legislativo 25 July 1998, n. 286 "Testo unico delle disposizioni concernenti la disciplina dell'immigrazione e norme sulla condizione dello straniero"

[49] DGR n. 5122 del 31.07.1997

[50] www.aslroma1.it/assistenza-sanitaria-ai-cittadini-extracomunitari.

[51] http://centroastalli.it/servizi/progetto-samifo/.

[52] DPR n.263/2012.

[53] http://www.miur.gov.it/web/guest/tematiche-e-servizi/istruzione-degli-adulti/integrazione-linguistica-e-sociale-degli-stranieri-adulti.

[54] www.tuttoscuola.com/istruzioni-per-luso-stato-regioni-enti-locali-un-sistema-integrato/.

[55] www.programmaintegra.it/wp/programma-integra/progetti/a-scuola-con-il-mondo/.

[56] www.ceisroma.it/upgrade/progetto-jambo/.

[57] www.programmaintegra.it/wp/programma-integra/progetti/.

References

Accorinti, M. (2013), *I fondi pubblici per l'integrazione degli immigrati*, Neodemos, http://briguglio.asgi.it/immigrazione-e-asilo/2013/ottobre/art-neodemos-accorinti.pdf.

Alexander, C. (2017), "Rome: from non-policy to delegation", in *Cities and Labour Immigration: Comparing Policy Responses in Amsterdam, Paris, Rome and Tel Aviv*, Routledge, London.

AMAR; Agenzia di Mediazione Abitativa di Roma (2014), *Valutazione finale progetto AMAR*, www.programmaintegra.it/wp/wp-content/uploads/2014/07/Report_valutazione_finale_AMAR.pdf.

Bakker, L., J. Dagevos and G. Engbersen (2013), "The importance of resources and security in the socio-economic integration of refugees. A study on the impact of length of stay in asylum accommodation and residence status on socio-economic integration for the four largest refugee groups in the NL", *Journal of International Migration and Integration*, pp. 431-448.

Boulant, J., M. Brezzi and P. Veneri (2016), "Income levels and inequality in metropolitan areas: A comparative approach in OECD countries"

Brezzi, M. et al. (2010), "Determinants of localisation of recent immigrants across OECD regions", OECD Workshop on Migration and Regional Development, 7 June 2010, OECD, Paris.

Cavasola, S. (2014), "L'offerta di servizi multiculturali del Comune di Roma", in *Osservatorio Romano sulle Migrazioni - Decimo Rapporto*, Edizioni IDOS, Rome.

Centro Studi e Ricerche IDOS (2016a), *Dossier Statistico Immigrazione 2016*, Edizioni IDOS, Rome.

Centro Studi e Ricerche IDOS (2016b), *Osservatorio Romano sulle Migrazioni. Undicesimo Rapporto*, Edizioni IDOS, Rome.

Centro Studi e Ricerche IDOS (2015), *Osservatorio Romano sulle Migrazioni. Decimo Rapporto*, Edizioni IDOS, Rome.

Chaloff, Jonathan (2006), "Innovating in the Supply of Services to Meet the Needs of Immigrants in Italy", in OECD, From Immigration to Integration: Local Solutions to a Global Challenge, OECD Publishing, Paris. https://doi.org/10.1787/9789264028968-6-en

Charbit, C. (2015), "Multi-level governance for migrant challenges", OECD, Paris.

Charbit, C. (2011), "Governance of public policies in decentralised contexts: The multi-level approach", *OECD Regional Development Working Papers*, No. 2011/04, OECD Publishing, Paris, http://dx.doi.org/10.1787/5kg883pkxkhc-en.

Charbit, C. and M. Michalun (2009), "Mind the gaps: Managing Mutual Dependence in Relations among Levels of Government", *OECD Working Papers on Public Governance*, No. 14, OECD Publishing, Paris. doi:10.1787/221253707200

CNEL (2013), *IX Rapporto sugli indici di integrazione degli immigrati in Italia*, http://briguglio.asgi.it/immigrazione-e-asilo/2013/luglio/sint-rapp-cnel-integr.pdf.

CNEL (2010), *VII Rapporto sugli indici di integrazione degli immigrati in Italia*,

Diaz Ramirez, M., T. Liebig, C. Thoreau and P. Veneri, (2017), "Assessing the integration of migrants in OECD regions", *OECD Regional Development Working Papers*, OECD Publishing, Paris, http://dx.doi.org/10.1787/fb089d9a-en.

Doctors Without Borders (2016), *Out of sight*, www.msf.org.za/system/tdf/publications/harmful_borders_def.pdf?file=1&type=node&id=7917.

Einaudi, L. (2007), *Le politiche dell'immigrazione in Italia dall'Unità ad oggi*, Laterza, Bari.

Fabbri, V. and M. Saggion (2014), "I rifugiati a Roma. I numeri dell'accoglienza, i percorsi di integrazione", in *Osservatorio Romano sulle Migrazioni - Nono Rapporto*, Edizioni IDOS, Rome.

Fabbri, V. (2016), "I richiedenti e titolari di protezione internazionale nella Capitale: presenze e percorsi", In *Osservatorio Romano sulle Migrazioni - Undicesimo Rapporto*, Edizioni IDOS, Rome.

Fioretti, C., S. Annunziata, F. Careri, A. Goni Mazzitelli, and D. Leone (2014), *Geografie dell'immigrazione nel Lazio. Territorio, Politiche, Attori. Primo rapporto dell'Unità di ricerca Roma Tre*, Cattedra UNESCO SSIIM, Venezia.

Gargiulo, E. (2013) "Le politiche di residenza in Italia: inclusione ed esclusione delle nuove cittadinanze locali", in *La governance dell'immigrazione. Diritti, politiche, competenze*, il Mulino, Bologna.

ISTAT (2018), *Cittadini non comunitari: presenza, nuovi ingressi e acquisizioni di cittadinanza*.

ISTAT (2017), Migrazioni internazionali e interne della popolazione residente Anno 2016, Novembre 2017, https://www.istat.it/it/files/2017/11/Report_Migrazioni_Anno_2016.pdf

ISTAT (2015), *Non Observed economy in national accounts*.

ISMU (2017) XXIII Rapporto sulle migrazioni, Fondazione ISMU.

Lunaria (2016), *Il mondo di dentro. Il sistema di accoglienza per richiedenti asilo e rifugiati a Roma*, www.lunaria.org/wp-content/uploads/2016/10/Il_mondo_di_dentro.pdf.

Ministry of Interior (2017), *The initiatives for good reception and integration of migrants in Italy*, www.interno.gov.it/sites/default/files/rapporto_annuale_buone_pratiche_di_accoglienza_2017_eng_web_rev1.pdf.

Ministry of Interior (2016), *Piano Nazionale di riapartizione*, www.mise.gov.it/images/stories/documenti/radio/PNRF_27_maggio_2015.pdf.

Ministry of Interior (2015a), *Italy's Roadmap*.

Ministry of Interior (2015b), *Rapporto sull'accoglienza di migranti e rifugiati in Italia*, www.asylumineurope.org/sites/default/files/resources/ministry_of_interior_report_on_reception_of_migrants_and_refugees_in_italy_october_2015.pdf.

Ministry of Labour and Social Policies (2017), *Newsletter December 2017*.

Ministry of Labour and Social Policies (2016), Analisi popolazione migrante.

Ministry of Labour and Social Policies (2016), *La presenza dei migranti nella città metropolitana di Roma Capitale*, Rapporto annuale 2016, www.integrazionemigranti.gov.it/Documenti-e-ricerche/Sintesi_RAM_DEF.pdf.

Ministry of Labour and Social Policies (2018), La presenza dei migranti nella città metropolitana di Roma Capitale, Rapporto annuale 2017, http://www.lavoro.gov.it/temi-e-priorita/immigrazione/Pagine/Studi-e-statistiche.aspx

Metropolitan City of Rome (2016), *Primo rapporto statistico sull'area metropolitana romana*, http://static.cittametropolitanaroma.gov.it/uploads/RapportovolumecompressoVER9216.pdf.

Roma Capitale (2017), Popolazione straniera residente Anno 2016 Anticipazione, https://www.comune.roma.it/web-resources/cms/documents/Popolazione_straniera_residente_2016_anticipazione.pdf

OECD (2018), *Working together for local integration of migrants and refugees*, OECD Publishing, Paris, http://dx.doi.org/10.1787/9789264085350-en.

OECD (2017), *International Migration Outlook*, OECD Publishing, Paris, http://dx.doi.org/10.1787/migr_outlook-2017-en.

OECD (2016), *Making integration work - Refugees and others in need of protection*, OECD Publishing, Paris, http://dx.doi.org/10.1787/9789264251236-en.

OECD (2014), *Jobs for immigrants Vol 4: labour market integration in Italy*, OECD Publishing, Paris, http://dx.doi.org/10.1787/9789264214712-en.

OECD (2006), *From Immigration to Integration: Local Solutions to a Global Challenge*, OECD Publishing, Paris, http://dx.doi.org/10.1787/9789264028968-en.

OECD and European Union (2015), *Indicators of Immigrant Integration 2015: Settling In*, OECD Publishing, Paris, http://dx.doi.org/10.1787/9789264234024-en.

Region of Lazio (2016), *Piano di intervento regionale*, www.integrazionemigranti.gov.it/leregioni/Documents/Piani%20di%20intervento%20FAMI/Marche_Piano%20di%20Intervento%20Regionale.pdf.

Natalia Ribas-Mateos (2010) How can we understand immigration in Southern Europe?, Journal of Ethnic and Migration Studies, 30:6, 1045-1063, DOI: 10.1080/1369183042000286241

Roman Observatory on Migrants (2016), *XI rapporto*.

SPRAR (2016a), *Rapporto sulla protezione internazionale in Italia, 2016*, www.cittalia.it/images/file/Rapporto%20protezione%20internazionale%202016.pdf.

SPRAR (2016b), *Manuale operativo per l'attivazione e la gestione di servizi di accoglienza e integrazione per richiedenti e titolari di protezione internazionale*, Servizio Centrale dello SPRAR, Rome, www.sprar.it/wp-content/uploads/2016/06/Documenti/Quaderni_servizio_centrale/manuale.pdf.

SPRAR (2014), *Rapporto sulla protezione internazionale in Italia, 2014*, www.cestim.it/argomenti/28rifugiati/2014_11_Rapporto_protezione_internazionale_in_italia_Sintesi.pdf.

UNSD (2017), "International migration statistics", United Nations Statistics Division, https://unstats.un.org/unsd/demographic/sconcerns/migration/migrmethods.htm#B.

Venanzetti, A. (2015), "Immigrati e apprendimento dell'italiano: cresce il disagio sociale nel Lazio", in *Osservatorio Romano sulle Migrazioni - Decimo Rapporto*, Edizioni IDOS, Rome.

Zolberg, A. R. (1987) "Wanted but Not Welcome: Alien Labor in Western Development," in *Population in an Interacting World*, Harvard University Press, Cambridge.

Additional Reading

Anpal Servizi - Ministero del lavoro e delle politiche sociali (2016), La presenza dei migranti nella città metropolitana di Roma Capitale - Rapporto annuale 2016, Roma.

Bettin, G. and Cela, E. (2014), L'evoluzione storica dei flussi migratori in Europa e in Italia, Cattedra UNESCO SSIIM, Venice.

Caponio, T. (2006), Città italiane e immigrazione. Discorso pubblico e politiche a Milano, Bologna e Napoli, Il Mulino, Bologna.

Centro Astalli (2017), Rapporto Annuale 2017, attività e servizi del Centro Astalli, Roma.

Cervelli, P. Cellamare, C. (2016), "La distribuzione spaziale delle principali popolazioni di immigrati della provincia di Roma in relazione ai processi di urbanizzazione", in Centro Studi e Ricerche IDOS, Osservatorio Romano sulle Migrazioni. Undicesimo Rapporto, Edizioni IDOS, Roma, pp. 44-49.

Cramerotti, R. (2016), "La popolazione straniera nella Città Metropolitana di Roma", in Centro Studi e Ricerche IDOS, Osservatorio Romano sulle Migrazioni. Undicesimo Rapporto, Edizioni IDOS, Roma.

Cremaschi, M. Fioretti, C. (2015), "Il Lazio e Roma metropolitana", in Balbo, M. (ed) Migrazioni e Piccoli Comuni, Franco Angeli, Milano.

European Union (2010), The European Social Fund: migrants and minorities - Summary Fiche, European Union.

Geraci, S. El Hamad, (2011) Migranti e accessibilità ai servizi sanitari: luci e ombre, in "Italian Journal of Public Health", Volume 8, Number 3, Suppl.3.

Giovannetti, M. Minicucci, C. (2016), "L'accoglienza nella rete del Sistema di protezione per richiedenti asilo e rifugiati nel Lazio", In Centro Studi e Ricerche IDOS, Osservatorio Romano sulle Migrazioni. Undicesimo Rapporto, Edizioni IDOS, Roma, p. 112-118.

Marcos Diaz Ramirez & Thomas Liebig & Cécile Thoreau & Paolo Veneri, 2018. "The integration of migrants in OECD regions: A first assessment," OECD Regional Development Working Papers 2018/01, OECD Publishing.

Ministero dell'Interno (2013), Integrazione:Conoscere, misurare, valutare, Roma

OECD (2014), Lavoro per gli immigrati: l'integrazione nel mercato del lavoro in Italia, OECD Publishing. http://dx.doi.org/10.1787/9789264216570-it.

OECD/UCLG (2016), Subnational Governments around the world: Structure and finance.

SPRAR (2015), Rapporto sulla protezione internazionale in Italia, 2015. ANCI, Caritas Italiana, Cittalia, Fondazione Migrantes, Servizio Centrale dello SPRAR and UNHCR, Roma.

http://www.altrodiritto.unifi.it/
http://www.asgi.it/
http://www.interno.gov.it/
http://www.meltingpot.org/
http://www.osservatoriomigranti.org/
http://www.sprar.it/
http://www.unhcr.com

Annex A. List of participants to the interviews with OECD delegation field visit March 22-24 2017

- Mr Andrea De Bonis, Mr Riccardo Clerici, Ms Laura Cantarini, Ms Nardos Neamin Office of UNHCR Rome
- Ms. Gabriella Sanna, Ms. Alice Dente and Ms. Alessandra Langellotti - Servizio Intercultura and Biblioteche di Roma
- Mr. Marco Wong - Associna
- Mr. Angelo Marano, Ms. Michela Micheli, Ms. Marcela Manyoma, Ms. Margherita Occhiuto, Dipartimento Politiche SocialiRoma Capitale
- Mr. Dante Sabatino, Researcher, Expert on migration policies, CNR IRPPS
- Mr. Filippo Gnolfo, ASL RM1, Regione Lazio, Local Health Offices, managed by the Lazio Region
- Ms. Sabina De Luca, Dipartimento Politiche e finanziamenti europei, Roma Capitale
- Mr. Lino Posteraro, CRI (Italian Red Cross) - Director of the Via Ramazzini Center
- Mr. Riccardo Compagnucci Former Prefect, for the transformation from PNA to SPRAR
- Mr. Salvatore Ippolito, AMIF, Co-ordinator Progetto Rimpatrio Volontario Assistito e Reintegrazione, AMIF.
- Ms. Ernesta Lombardi, Dipartimento Politiche Abitative Roma Capitale Responsible for popular housing system.
- Ms. Stefania Wyss e Massimiliano Ostuni, Dip.to Turismo, Formazione e Lavoro Roma Capitale
- Ms. Stefania Congia, Ministero del Lavoro e delle Politiche Sociali
- Mr Catello Caiazzo, Camera di commercio
- Ms. Valentina Fabbri, President Cooperativa INTEGRA
- Mr. Lorenzo Chialastri, Caritas
- Simone Andreotti Cooperativa INmigrazione
- Cecilia Pani, Comunitá St Egidio
- Emanuele Selleri, Casa Scalabrini
- Camillo Ripamonti, Centro Astalli
- Mr Francesco DÁmuri, Bank of Italy
- Ms Donatella Terni, ANCI
- Vice Prefetto Ms. Martha Matscher, Ministero dell'Interno - Dipartimento per le Libertà Civili e per L'immigrazione

Annex B. National legislative framework for Migration and Asylum

1986	L. 943/1986 Foschi law
1990	L.39/1990 Martelli law, which norms the right of asylum
1992	L.91/1992 Law on citizenship
1993	L.205/1993 Mancino law against discrimination for racial or ethnic reasons; Law proposal of the Contri commission on regularization, to review the Martelli law
1995	L. 563/1995 Puglia law to tackle illegal migration; L.489/1995 Dini decree, introducing a new amnesty for irregular migrant, and new norms on expulsions of illegal migrants
1998	L.40/1998 Turco-Napolitano law, that became Testo Unico sull'Immigrazione DLgs. 246-1998, establishing the main guidelines for public policy on migration in Italy, in terms of programming migratory flows, tackling illegal immigration, promoting a wide series of rights for the integration of regular migrants. It established a national fund for immigrants integration, and gives to local administrations (regions, municipalities) crucial roles for immigrants integration. For instance this law established (art 43) that foreign citizens with a permit of stay of at least two years with a regular work could access on the same conditions as Italian citizens public housing and mediation services offered by social agencies.
2002	L.189/2002 Bossi-Fini Law, it is a partial revision of the Turco-Napolitano especially for what concerns the opposition to illegal immigration. Major innovations are: measures which limit the possibilities of entrance in Italy, fusion of the national funds for migration with the one of social policy, criminalization of illegal migrants and introduction of Centres for identification and expulsion (CIE). It introduced a new amnesty for irregular migrants working in caregiving.
2007	Law-design Amato-Ferrero to introduce the principle of citizenship for ius solis. It never became law
2008	L.125/2008 and L.94/2009, Maroni security package. Introduction of the Integration Agreement. Signed between the migrant and the Italian State it foresees bilateral engagements and it establishes the condition for renovating the residence permit.
2001-2014	Series of decrees aimed at modifying existing normative to include in the Italian regulative system some important european dispositions (e.g. 2009/50/CE and 2009/52/CE)
2017	DL. 13/2017, Minniti decree on international protection and contrast to illegal immigration. It introduces measures for speeding up the administrative and jurisdictional procedures in terms of international protection and it introduces measures to ease the operation of identification of extra-EU migrants and to fight illegal immigration. Law proposal 'Ius Soli': the Italian Parliament rejected a law proposal, which would have allowed children born in Italy to non-Italians who have long-term residency permits, or who arrive before their 12th birthdays and spend at least five years in formal education, to obtain a passport.
2018	D.L 113/2018 art. 1 the "Security decree" (Decreto sicurezza) introduced several changes to the asylum legislative framework, among others it revoked the possibility to issue termporary permits (two years) based on humanitarian reasons.

ORGANISATION FOR ECONOMIC CO-OPERATION AND DEVELOPMENT

The OECD is a unique forum where governments work together to address the economic, social and environmental challenges of globalisation. The OECD is also at the forefront of efforts to understand and to help governments respond to new developments and concerns, such as corporate governance, the information economy and the challenges of an ageing population. The Organisation provides a setting where governments can compare policy experiences, seek answers to common problems, identify good practice and work to co-ordinate domestic and international policies.

The OECD member countries are: Australia, Austria, Belgium, Canada, Chile, the Czech Republic, Denmark, Estonia, Finland, France, Germany, Greece, Hungary, Iceland, Ireland, Israel, Italy, Japan, Korea, Latvia, Lithuania, Luxembourg, Mexico, the Netherlands, New Zealand, Norway, Poland, Portugal, the Slovak Republic, Slovenia, Spain, Sweden, Switzerland, Turkey, the United Kingdom and the United States. The European Union takes part in the work of the OECD.

OECD Publishing disseminates widely the results of the Organisation's statistics gathering and research on economic, social and environmental issues, as well as the conventions, guidelines and standards agreed by its members.

www.ingramcontent.com/pod-product-compliance
Lightning Source LLC
LaVergne TN
LVHW061947070526
838199LV00060B/4012